Al Westbrook

MY DADDY USED TO SAY....

The lighter side of outdoor sports

By Al Westbrook

My daddy used to say, "There's no point in being a fool if you can't prove it now and again!"

Published by the Westbrook Family

Bellmore, New York

First Edition

First Printing + 750 + 1996

Additional copies may be obtained by sending a
check for $10.00

(includes postage and all tax)

For your convenience, an order form

is provided at the back of this book

ISBN 1-57502-200-1

Printed in the USA by

3212 E. Hwy 30
Kearney, NE 68847
800-650-7888

It is with much gratitude that I dedicate this book to The Nassau County Fish and Game Association, under the capable and amazing leadership of Sherwin E. Allen, Esq., where I had the great, good fortune to act as Editor for sixteen years, and most especially to Vic Gajan, my hunting partner, for not only planting the seed for this book, but watering and nurturing from time to time, until, stubbornly, it grew.

Forward:

The outdoors could be a courtyard in Brooklyn, New York or a patch of mountain peak in Bozeman, Montana. What I mean to say is there are degrees of outdoors. I've always taken my outdoors straight up and use every opportunity to dive right into it.

I'm at home with a fly rod or a shotgun, camera, or field glasses; makes little difference, as long as all God's creatures, large and small, allow me to be a part of their ongoing saga. A saga, I might add, of which they are sadly unaware.

This humble collection of snapshots of outdoor adventures, I hope, will give as much pleasure to the reader as it did me to affix them on paper.

CONTENTS

MY DADDY USED TO SAY

By
Al Westbrook

CHAPTER 1

FIND THE HAT

It's crossed my mind before that sportsmen
are a peculiar lot, given today's standards.
Their sights are usually set slightly high and
to the right of the usual new car every three
years and a fancy home complete with in-ground
pool. They spend much time dreaming of the
great outdoors and somehow are guiltless in
leaving the long overdue paint job for a while
in lieu of a hunting or fishing excursion.

On the other hand he (or she), is subject to
some of the same pressures as the rest of
society and for funds, must wo...wor...work.
Sorry, but its just hard for me to say. Now if
employment could be found such as testing new
fishing rods or camping gear there would be
little problem. However, for most of us,
including my good friend and comrade from
boyhood, Benchley Kane, more mundane tasks
await.

Bench found his niche with a company that
makes some kind of fork truck like thing. Bench

sells these whatever-they-ares. Fact is he's
probably good at it because he's always running
off somewhere or other just a sellin' up a
storm. Hence we come to the point of the saga.

Now I've known some avid fishermen in my
time but Bench makes them pall in comparison.
It's been said that he doesn't go as far as the
mailbox without a fold-up rod and some tackle.

Just last spring my friend was on assignment
to an obscure area in Wyoming with great
anticipation of foisting more of those fork
truck things on the embryonic industry there.
Every day as he made his calls he had to drive
past some of the most inviting wild streams
imaginable. Naturally Bench was tardy on
occasion and arrived with a splotch or two of
mud on his shoes after an impromptu visit with
some trout. The people he visited never let an
opportunity go to mention the *really* good
fishing to be had further up in the mountains.
This of course was like waving a lemon meringue
pie in front of a dieter. It gave our good ol'
boy an idea.

Under the pretext of delivering a status
report on how the sales trip was going he phoned
his immediate supervisor. "Say, Cal, how's it
going back there?"

"Yeah, I've got some good leads here," Bench
reported. "By the way, bein' as how I'll be
here awhile longer and with the weekend holiday,
and me bein' a fisherman and all, what do you
say to the company springin' for a little
fishing trip for me, say Saturday?"

Cal apparently stifled the usual management
chuckle reserved for such requests. He did
admit that although he thought the idea absurd
he'd ask Bert Dolan for an o.k. This was a
terrific idea since Bert was an avid angler also
(a factoid not known by Cal or he'd surely have

asked someone else). Considering there were at
least seventeen equally qualified bosses to ask
who could turn it down, this was a lucky break.
A phone call next day disclosed, "Permission
Granted."

When Bench got back to New York, over a few
wee sips of golden elixir, he told me of the
most fantastic natural trout fishing I'd ever
heard. He described scenes that would make your
blood run cold. He told of craggy mountain drop
offs above idyllic raging streams, winds of
nearly fifty miles an hour roaring down a canyon
where the pools were practically aboil with
rainbow and cutthroat trout, and icy cold riffle
and pocket water harboring golden browns. With
ensuing goblets of the nectar the volume grew
but the believability diminished. I sure did
envy the old son of a gun.

Not one week later I met him once more and
he mentioned a further development in his GREAT
FISHING TRIP. Well, I certainly had to hear
this and besides it was a super excuse to linger
awhile at *Clancy's* and release some more of that
wonderful liquid all cramped up and capped in
those confining bottles; to *Clancy's* fine tavern
we did go.

Seems Bench turned in his expense report as
usual; the only exception being the inclusion of
the aforenoted GREAT FISHING TRIP. He had the
usual list of items including meals, laundry,
room and board, etc. Then at the bottom
itemized carefully was:

Fishing Trip:

Transportation	$41.65
Guide Services	$100.50
Fishing Hat	$9.95

He allowed as how he had contracted a very
knowledgeable guide and his success with the

fish was offered as proof. In fact on the
morning of their departure it looked a bit
tricky in the sky and the guide suggested before
they leave town he purchase something to cover
his dome. Apparently the rain to come would not
last long but while it was at it, had the great
potential to soak one through.

The advice was taken and as projected,
torrential rains came but were short lived, as
advertised. Well anyway, his expense reports
are, it turns out, not reviewed by Mr. Dolan,
the fisherman, but by Mr. Franklin who wouldn't
know a trout from a snake. His report was
returned with a grand black stamp that simply
stated, "DISAPPROVED". The darkness and obvious
smudging of the large letters showed it was
stamped with apparent glee.

A note affixed to the report read: "I've
spoken to Mr. Dolan and I can see where
transportation is a necessity for "that trip"
and whereas most fishermen probably can't find
fish at the supermarket, let alone in their
natural domain, I suspect the guide would also
be indispensable. But, Mr. Kane, in no possible
search of my imagination can I see where the
Company should pay for a fishing hat! I
therefore request on behalf of the Company
(which has been more than lenient in this case,
I'm sure you'll agree), that you submit a
corrected report."

Bench never did take a liking to old man
Franklin. In his younger days Bench would have
reached the Appellate Division over the matter
but, mellowed and wizened with time, he simply
drew up a new report. That is not to say he had
given up; no sir. The tabulations were somewhat
modified and set down in order and again at the
bottom:

Fishing Trip:
  Transportation $41.65
  Guide Services $100.50

The rest of the mundane report had also been revised to a small degree such that the grand total on line 37 box 4 next to his signature remained mysteriously identical to the first report. A note affixed to the report read: "See if you can find the hat!"

My Daddy used to say, "Things don't always appear as they are, they're generally a lot worse."

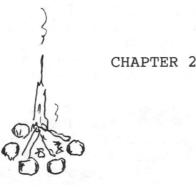

CHAPTER 2

THE CAMP COOK

I don't care if you're camping, fishing, or hunting, there's an indispensable character in your midst called the 'camp cook'. Oh, sure, now I mention it and you all remember him but when he was doing his thing, if he was good, you've forgotten him and if he wasn't, nobody's heard of him since!

Fact is a camp cook's popularity lasts only one third of a day and then, as they say, he's got to earn his wings all over again. And when you are tempted to chastise our hero about his last serving of mystery meat, consider the budget presented to the typical camp cook. He often gets left over toll money and bottle redemption funds to work with. This generally means precious food leftovers must be miserly retained. They are often very handy for lunches but if the camp cook looks in the cooler and offers, "Who wants the brown lunch and who wants the green?", you can expect some trouble.

Another thing to be leery of is a camp cook that grins. Grinning is not normal. A chef in a sportsman's camp has no reason to grin other than mischief. So, if grinning, he places an

unrecognizable mound of hoopla in front of you
and steps back observing, it's a great time to
recall a task that simply must be done
immediately, and wait for someone else to dig
in. You may find out that suddenly everyone has
something to do.

But remember, volunteers are few and far
between so I suggest a major dampening of
comments about the efforts of the one you've got
'cause once in the woods if he goes on strike,
management, so to speak, will select another.
This is seldom a democratic event and typically
turns out to be the smallest, youngest, or, all
else being equal, the one who complained the
most. There is rarely any consideration of
qualifications.

Also, it's a good idea to keep in mind that
you are not at the Conrad Hilton on these
outdoor jaunts. You'll have to give a little.
Say, when the camp cook substitutes chili in
place of the oyster stew and instead of the
usual Caesar's salad you again get chili, it's
most likely just a temporary concession to the
lack of accouterments. And if you begin to
wonder at the magic used to turn a steak into
charcoal, recollect that it's hard to set a camp
fire to 350 degrees for any predictable length
of time. In fact, most camp fires zing right
through 350 degrees on their way to about a
thousand degrees in a twinkling.

My own camp cook also doubles as my son so
there are certain limits and restrictions put on
the behavior of both sides. After several
seasons, though, I must give him credit. He's
learning to do a minute steak in roughly thirty
seconds and he can now fish a hot dog out of the
ashes, dust it off and get it back on the grill
without so much as interrupting the current
conversation. Says it's all in the wrist.

My Daddy used to say, "If you're a camp cook and can't satisfy a hungry bunch of sportsmen you can kiss your axe goodbye!"

CHAPTER 3

A FISH(Y) STORY

Now I'll have to admit I've heard some wild fish stories in my day and, in fact, been a party to some. The ethic of catch and release has, fortunately, caught on, at least in fly fishing circles, so we'll be able to fish another day. However, without the evidence, so to speak, the door is left wide open for exaggeration expanded even greater than before. Nothing in recorded history has furthered the cause of the fish story more than catch and release. Without fish or picture of same, the audience in a fish tale is expected to believe the teller explicitly based on reputation alone. If the listener happens to be another fisherman, there's no problem; he'll get his chance soon enough.

The definition of 'catch' blurs somewhat when the requirement of having the actual fish in the creel disappears. Whereas one could not claim a fish that breaks off at the net, prior to the new ethic, now one can claim that it was simply the 'release' in catch and release. By logical extension, a fish that never even breaks the surface could easily fit that category too.

On a very slow fishing day a 'hit' might be
considered a fish that *would* have been released
had he indeed been hooked, played and landed.
Therefore, in the absence of a bonafide catch,
and using a very free interpretation of catch
and release, such a fish would be in the tally.

And when it comes to the weight of fish in a
fish story, there was always great latitude
here. I've noticed fish perpetually come in one
pound, or at the very most, one half-pound
increments. How often has your buddy showed you
a picture of his catch and claimed it was a
'three pounder'. Maybe he will say, "Brought
home a four and a half pound bass too, but
didn't get a picture; ran out of film." Such
descriptions fit the fisherman's lexicon
exactly. Estimates to the nearest pound or
half-pound are always accepted as accurate and
seldom questioned; *never* questioned by another
angler for sure. The very minute a person
gathers fishing gear, approaches the pond, river
or stream, and accepts the mantle of
'fisherman', he, or she, automatically absorbs
the unfailing talent for accurately determining
the weight of a fish, albeit to he nearest pound
at least. Note that you'll never hear, "I
caught a nice two pound, six ounce rainbow
yesterday." Nope, to do this would tend to cast
doubt on all previous announcements rounded off
to the normal pound or half-pound. Such a
fisherman would certainly be ostracized and
invited to tell his story walking.

The length of a fish has the same perplexing
characteristic of never violating the inch,
half-inch rule. Other fishermen understand this
standard and will not challenge its seemingly
amazing infringement on nature. No matter, when
it's his turn to relate his experience astream,
fish are also stretched by even inches, for

clarity of course. Such are the rudimentary
guidelines for the typical fish story.

Size and weight aside, there are other fish
tales which might seem...well...fishy. The day
I met Henry was just such a not so typical
fish(y) tale. Although some may be tempted to
doubt the veracity of the tale, I'm sure all
will recognize it for what it is; whatever that
is.

The story begins on a idyllic see-your-
breath morning in April. I had worked some
overtime the day before to reduce the guilt
burden of taking this day off for a fishing
excursion. I was even able to ignore the "how
can you do this to us" looks from fellow
workers. Actually this was made easy by the
boss declaring that, given my contribution to
the collective effort, they would get along.
It's nice to have support.

So finally there I was, absolutely alone at
streamside. My first cast was unnoteworthy and
typical which means my fly caught a bush on the
back cast and cost me one hand-tied fly. My
pals call these patented casts 'snicks' because
that's the sound my little clippers make as I
cut the leader from the bush, tree, or hat. The
day progressed in this same wonderful fashion
and by late afternoon I had miraculously caught
three rather ordinary fish, but keepers
nonetheless. I had planned a trout dinner and
felt three fish was just about right. I did
catch and release a number of others but I still
love a trout dinner once in a while. That's
when I met Henry.

This fellow was parked right behind my truck
as I arrived at the road. The back seat of his
car was just jammed with shiny, new fishing
gear, some of it still sporting the store sales
tags. Out steps this gent about six foot

thirteen and from the other side of the car, looking a bit impatient, a very unforgettable blonde woman, thankfully a bit shorter. He introduced himself as Henry Novack and offered me ten dollars apiece for my catch. Normally this would have been met with repugnance but my conscience lost the battle when I realized that thirty bucks would pay for gas, lunch and the dozen or so snicks. Besides, who'd believe I caught three fish anyway?

The story so far is unremarkable until a week later I stopped at the bank, once more to delete my shrinking funds, and stepped up to the window. At once I recognized the gorgeous blonde on the other side and I boomed out with a friendly, "Howdy Mrs. Novack! How's the fishing?" At which time the rest of the tellers and other folks back there that do bank stuff seemed to be simultaneously overcome by some severe debilitating malady as they fell to the floor coughing, choking and clutching their mouths. As they doubled over and slid from my view, Mrs. Novack, through clenched teeth and curled lip, said in a whisper, "I am NOT Mrs. Novack and furthermore I HATE fishing." She further expostulated, "And Henry HATES fishing too. However," she continued quietly, "Mrs. Novack tells me he loves it." Then in a bigger voice tumbling over a typical teller's smile she queried, "Will that be all sir?"

My Daddy wouldn't have anything to say about this.

CHAPTER 4

MEANNESS

Sportsmen as a group aren't mean at all.
Oh, certainly there's a temporary mean thought
when the boss says you've got to work Saturday
even though he knows full well that you've
planned a pip of a fishing weekend. But other
than that fleeting instance or two, sportsmen
are basically smilers and laughers at heart.

Partly, the reason for this is because they
got exposed to meanness early in life. My own
experience may serve as a workable example.

Me and Blinky Rheinhardt used to love to
fish Browning's Creek after school but by the
time we walked the three miles home (my own lads
to this day refuse to believe my three mile walk
to school every day, rain or shine), fishing
time was at a premium. This meant only one
thing; we had to take a short cut through Mrs.
McGonagle's place. There was a clear route
between the fence in the pen where she kept
about 900,000 chickens, it seemed to us, and her
barn. Most times we could blitz right through
trailing two cans of worms, poles with hooks
dangling in wild circles and sometimes a sack
containing a snack like two peanut butter and

banana sandwiches, a couple of left over
breakfast rolls, a box of vanilla wafers, four
or five apples and several slices of pickle.
We'd start with a "ready", "set", "go". and
churn up the barnyard on whirling feet, covered
in sneakers (the kind with the round circles at
each ankle) that barely touched the ground.

There were times though that Mrs. McGonagle
would magically appear at the far edge of the
barn waving a broom and come charging right down
on us. I don't know if you've ever seen
sneakers smoke to a stop and do a mid air one-
eighty degree reversal, restart, and accelerate
in a split second scarcely touching the earth.
Well it was common back when I was a kid and
Mrs. McGonagle was around. We practiced the
maneuver often just to be ready. In fact I wore
out Mom's parlor rug (now referred to as
'carpet' for crimminy sakes) in just a few
practice sessions 'cause when the sneaks did
touch ground eventually it looked a lot like a
Boeing 747 landing.

Yep, that Mrs. McGonagle was a mean one by
golly but Jeeesum Crow! she didn't half measure
up to my own Gandma W.

Grams owned a potato and pumpkin farm on
Long Island (they were taters and punkins in
those days). My sister and I used to get the
biggest pumpkins for Halloween for jack-o-
lanterns. However there were some folks who
tried to help themselves to Gram's 'punkins' and
then she'd get mean.

Grams would stand guard with her shotgun in
a way that made Mrs. McGonagle's effort pall in
comparison. Grandma W. thought death was
entirely too good for those rapscatrallions, as
she called 'em. So, she loaded the shells with
rock salt instead of the little metal balls. My
sister and I used to stand by the porch window

in relative safety and be richly entertained by
Grams dusting the crooks with her own brand of
justice. I was never surprised by the quick
smoking stop, mid-air reversal, and lightning
acceleration of the sneakers with the little
circles on the ankles, having done the
performance many times, but sis never ceased to
be awed by the act. Of course the rock salt
usually added a colorful verbal addition to the
gymnastics.

Now Grandma W. might have been high on the
list of meanies but by far the best in that
category was old Lyle Halffeather. Old Lyle,
part Injun we were told, had a look that'd stop
a train goin' down a three mile grade. We were
all scared of Old Lyle, more than getting caught
in the dark even! He owned a large spread that
just happened to have a great beaver pond on it.
The pond was reportedly swarming with perch,
sunnies and bass as big as goats.

Lyle always seemed to be around his tarpaper
shack so we just couldn't manage to sneak in to
do some fishing. And talk about mean, it was
publicly known that mean man Halffeather had
imported killer hornets and set them up all
around the pond; everybody knew that. We
weren't scared of *them* but we sure were of mean
man Halffeather.

Well we'd heard from folks around that Old
Lyle needed his daily "medicine" and judging by
the way their eyes rolled up to the sky when
they said it we figured his condition was pretty
serious. In fact we could see hundreds of large
medicine jugs around his shack. We guessed
there's got to be a time when he had to refill
his prescriptions. We agreed to case the place
and sure enough we found out when Old Lyle went
to town. The plan was to sneak in to the pond,
catch a quick months supply of sunnies, a couple

of big bass the size of a Buick and beat it out
of there before mean man Halffeather got back.
     Things went well at first and we approached
the pond fearful now only of those killer
hornets which for some reason were nowhere to be
seen. Celebrating our good fortune with a first
cast, our lines had barely slapped the water
when we heard Old Lyle's battered old car
sputter to a stop. Not sixty seconds later we
heard mean man Halffeather shouting, "Hey you
varmints, git away from that thar pond! Or else
I'll sick ma killer hornets on ya!"
     We ran like the dickens, leaving small
swatches of clothing on sticker bushes and
actually left streaks in the air where no bushes
were in the way. We once again celebrated our
good fortune at merely losing a couple of
fishing poles and bits of skin in places that
were insignificant.
     A year later the great puzzle of how mean
man Halffeather knew we were fishing his pond
got the better of me. I mentioned the incident
to my Dad; admitting having fished the forbidden
Halffeather pond. Dad, fortunately for me,
could handle a tale like that and commenced
laughing so hard I worried for his health. I
was pleased he saw the humor in the thing and
then, with tears of mirth angling from his eyes
to the stubble on his cheeks, he explained.
"Poor old Lyle's had a few too many scrimmages
without a helmet," he said, "but he ain't dumb!
Every day after his trip to town, he goes back
behind his shack a yells, 'Hey you varmints, git
away from that thar pond!'"
     My Daddy used to say, "I knew a man so mean
he'd train homing pigeons......and move."

CHAPTER 5

I BELIEVE IN SANTA
(but my wife doesn't)

It was just a few years ago when this absolutely true, honest Injun story occurred. It was Christmas Eve, in fact at exactly twelve midnight when I showed up at the cabin door to meet my family for a Christmas celebration. This is the time of year that sportsmen dream not of sugar plums but new Remington's and Orvis fishing sticks. The weather was frightful and my cheeks rosy. I smelled faintly of gasoline, the wherefores to be explained shortly, and *not* Jim Beam as my wife claimed with stubborn certainty.

My spouse of some twenty plus years actually accused me of lingering at *Clancy's* instead of prudently hitting the road after a day of waterfowling. I had stolen one day, *one day* mind you, to shoot some birds with a few buddies after which I was to drive the two hundred and fifty miles to our cabin to join the family. Well, my wife's accusations not withstanding, I did make it to the cabin bringing my old Jeep truck to a begrudging halt, staggered to the door from, sheer exhaustion, and began to relate, with the very last of my strength, the actual, incredible story.

I had spent the day hunting with four good friends and finished the day with two birds at about four in the afternoon. My intentions were to rush to my bride of two decades with all due haste as I also missed my two wonderful sons whom I had not seen in a whole twenty-four hours. But my comrades would not have it.. *No*! Not without a toast on Christmas Eve; merries and happies all around. So I relented and we gathered at *Clancy's*; me for just one mug of spring water, then on the road to my darling mate and my two youngsters. And so I did, yesiree!

When we entered *Clancy's* emporium the merriment almost erased the memory of the snow flurries outside. When I left, which could have been no more than a mere matter of minutes, as I recollect, it was snowing gayly and the wind had somehow grown to alarming proportions.

My trusty Jeep and I had gone less than half the distance when the storm, which I first thought looked pretty, turned into a full howl blizzard. I beseeched whatever gods may be to turn off the snow machine in the sky.

My C.B. radio brought no response and indeed there was no one else on the highway at all. I peered down at the rectangular hole in the dashboard where the old A.M. radio should have been, and was, until a few days ago, when I removed it for repair. That's when I spied the bright yellow carton on the floor containing the new fuel filter I had been meaning to install. I'd had several warnings and yet I simply forgot.

As if on cue the Jeep sputtered once and died. Silence, nothing, no gas in the old carburetor. There I was, stuck in the middle of

a deserted road in a raging storm when all of a
sudden a vehicle with little beady lights showed
in the distance. As it approached, I spotted a
second vehicle, larger and with a bunch of
lights, way behind the first. With visibility
about nil, I prayed both would see my plight in
time.

As the first fellow approached it turned out
to be a big, shiny, red tow truck driven by an
elderly gent who stopped just behind me, got
out, hung a few big bumperettes over his front
bumper and gestured for me to steer the Jeep off
the road. He nudged my aging truck to the side
just seconds before a mammoth wing plow
descended on the spot where my truck stalled and
whooshed by without slowing so much as one
scintilla!

After a few dazzled moments I turned to
thank the old fellow but he had already stuffed
the bumperettes in a white sack slung over his
shoulder as he headed to his red tow truck. As
he jumped up to the cab with his long white
beard blowing in the tempest and one hand
clamping down his tasseled, red, wool cap I
noticed he wore a bright, red, one piece hunting
suit with a wide black belt and black boots.

He had already begun to pull out onto the
highway as I reached the tow truck to thank him
properly. I'm not even sure if he heard me as
all he said was he was in a bit of a hurry; had
many stops to make and must be done by midnight.
That's when I saw the great pile of gift wrapped
packages lashed to the back of the tow truck
under a tarpaulin. In fact the load took up the
entire rear deck.

Over the din of the blizzard I heard him
shout something about a "Merry Christmas to all
and to all a good night!". as he waved his big
hand out the cab window. The truck roared off

into the darkness; the loose tow chains sounding very much like bells on a sleigh.

I managed to change the filter, spilling some gasoline on my clothes, and my guess was luckily correct, that was the problem. The truck ran well the rest of the trip. I arrived at the cabin weary and fuel soiled but cheered by the sight of my lovely wife and two boys. And that's the truth. You can even call my chums at *Clancy's* and they'll tell you (they'd better!)

When this story comes up now and again, my charming betrothed always asks why, while I drove the distance in a "ferocious storm", was there only a half inch of snow around the cabin? And I truly can't answer that one; I figure that must be part of the miracle.

To a Christmas story like this one my Daddy would say only, "HO...HO...HO."

CHAPTER 6

THE FIB

The Fib is a very versatile tool. You'll
find it in almost every tackle box, in each
hunter's pack and often simply in the hip pocket
kept at the ready to be pulled out and used if
necessary. I hasten to point out, though, that
I recommend its use as a defensive weapon only.
The Fib can be used to provide cover for poor
memory as in, "How many points did last year's
buck have?" It has the usual application of
countering a previous Fib hurled across during a
discussion with other sportsmen. Further,
producing the Fib at the proper moment is useful
in stopping the "long-and-boring story"
sometimes encountered in camp.

Fibs, handy as they are, should be brief and
restrained as their purpose is not amusement but
rather the mild insertion of awe. If the Fib
produces mirth it has been fabricated beyond the
legal limits or has been incorrectly executed.
There are unwritten limits beyond which the
fibber will lose credibility and perhaps produce
the unwanted comedic reaction. This is to be
avoided at all costs if the Fib is ever to be
employed again in the company of those same

sportsmen. For instance a fisherman is
certainly allowed, nay expected, to add
approximately 10% to the weight of an average
catch. A really spectacular fish may permit up
to, say, 15% but no more. The hunter may add
one bird per trip to his bag and no greater than
twenty pounds to his buck's dressed weight.
Most of these apparent errors can be explained
in reality by loss to evaporating moisture or
perhaps meat scraped off by careless skinning or
a particularly difficult drag. Blurred vision
from the strain of the hunt can account for a
point or two on a whitetail rack.

I myself never employ the Fib. Firstly,
because at the age of five my mother told me if
I did, my tongue would turn purple and fall off.
Secondly, logic dictates you can't add ounces to
a fish yet to be caught or points to your buck's
rack that is still happily roaming the woods.

I did once make an exception, my mother's
entreaty notwithstanding, and took a chance on
the Fib. I was clamped securely in a headlock
performed by Big Ralph, my fourth grade nemesis.
In order to prevent permanent indentation of my
Adam's apple I indicated that I had not removed
a Baby Ruth from his lunch sack. As soon as he
let up and my eyeballs snapped back in place
from their position two inches down my cheeks, I
hurriedly dropped the crushed candy wrapper
behind my back and hoped I had covered it
sufficiently with my boot. Ralphie, not too
bright (in fact I've heard of people who don't
know anything but Ralphie didn't even *suspect*),
did not question why I did not move from that
spot all afternoon.

We had been fishing Browning's Pond that
Saturday. Big Ralph left his lunch sack on a
rock in the sun right next to the place I
eventually picked to sit while I fished. I do

believe in fate and have offered this as the
reason the lunch sack and I were on the same
rock that day. Others have claimed it had more
to do with my being able to smell a peanut
butter sandwich a half mile away. Whatever.

I began to think Ralphie could have
something in there that might spoil and wouldn't
he be proud of me for saving it from devastation
by moving it to the shade? Actually this was
unlikely as we kids never had anything but
peanut butter sandwiches and every kid knows
anything that happens to peanut butter
sandwiches on a fishing trip when you're hungry
merely enhances its delicacy. Anyway, I
unfurled the top of the brown bag and out
tumbled a Baby Ruth! A Baby Ruth!

We would get twenty cents approximately once
each month for the Saturday movie plus a nickel
for a Baby Ruth. Ralphie had either A)robbed a
bank, B)done some incredibly good deed to
deserve such a reward (note: B) is not a real
choice), or C)he had saved the candy and not
eaten it at the movies. I had little time for
further speculation.

In point of fact, however, I had not *removed*
the candy from the sack, it *fell* out. And
landing on the hot sunny rock was not a good
place for a Baby Ruth. So, deciding that the
greater sin would be to permit this special
treat to dribble down the side of an
unappreciative rock, I sort of corrected the
problem.

But the Fib, as I say, is more often
employed to correct the measurements of a fish
that shrunk at the dock while waiting for the
scale and ruler. Or that six...er...eight
pointer you took last hunting season on the edge
of the one hun... er... two hundred foot ledge.
It's nearly certain that animal lost two, maybe

four points in the fall and drag to the truck
through the blinding snowstorm and with your bad
leg and all. A Fib can sure dress up an
otherwise dull story.

The defensive application might go something
like this. Say a bunch of the boys are ticking
away a Friday night at *Clancy's* over a glass or
two of Old Sniggler. Big Ralph, now older and
even bigger but no brighter, has the audacity to
bring up for discussion our last trip to Lake
Tepper where I'd had better than my usual luck
and landed a fish in the one and a half pound
range. Ralphie's couldn't have been more than a
pound but as he recollects, it was one pound
nine ounces. I then casually mention, "Oh,
yeah, that's the time I caught the two pound
trout."

He will then say, "Wow! did I say *one* pound
nine ounces? I meant *two* pounds nine ounces,
har, har!" This is a perfectly acceptable
exchange of Fibs.

As is the application in this typical
situation. You are waiting for a bus...Up steps
what appears to be a stranger but turns out to
be Bob Benson, your neighbor down the road.
"Oh, hey whaddya say?", says Bob, whom you
haven't seen in a while.

"How's it goin' Bob, what's up?", you reply,
trying to give off an aura of total cool.

Bob then says casually, "Hey remember that
pheasant hunt last year?", in order to open the
door to mention he bagged two birds. You know
it was one bird and counter with, "Almost caught
up to my three birds, eh Bob?" All this is
legal parry, permitted and accepted, that is as
long as you can put up with your fellow bus
riders blowing noises through their lips at both
of you.

It should be realized that it is not always necessary to resort to the Fib. For the purpose of example, jut last season I was casting to a difficult pool on Cobble Creek. The pool looked promising but was under heavy hanging branches requiring an expert side cast of maybe sixty feet. The fly had to be delicately presented over a log bristling with stubby broken limbs and dropped just short of a stand of Devil's club.

I made the cast precisely on target with a graceful peeling arc causing only the merest "pffft" as it landed. I was rewarded almost immediately with a hit from a big rainbow trout and I deftly set the hook. I then cajoled him, while in mid leap to jump the log and brought him to net after about ten minutes of expert maneuvering. I'll admit to some difficulty in lifting the rascal to the creel as his great heft was a true surprise.

I hope it's evident that the Fib is not required for an absolutely-true-in-every-detail story like this. Uh...wait a sec here...I think I've got to go. Something wrong with my tongue; looks like it's maybe turning purple! Feels like it might fall off!

My Daddy used to say, "An apple a day keeps the doctor away. A Fib a day could keep everybody away."

CHAPTER 7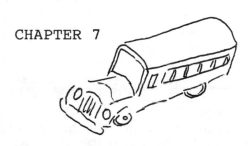

THE GOOD DEED

It's not too infrequent that my wife will
voice her opinion that I, that is *me*, am very
selfish. She will point out that I spend too
much time cavorting to streams and lakes to fish
and too much time, money and everything else on
hunting, "For crimminy sakes!", if I may use an
exact quote.

"You think only of yourself!", she will
incorrectly assess.

I counter with expertly exposed truth that
we often do things together such as fishing,
crosscountry skiing, grocery shopping and other
wild adventures. These bouts of criminal
accusation, I've noticed in the twenty plus
years of our just less than blissful marriage,
tend to precede a request for new shoes, a
"darling" dress or after the uncovering of a
significant modification to the fenders on the
family sedan. She has steadfastly, and I
maintain stubbornly, refused to alter her
opinion regardless of the clear and poignant
examples of my obvious unselfishness. I offer,
only for purposes of illustration, for instance,
the marvelous Remington 700 rifle I gave her for

Christmas last year. She feigns ignorance of
the great sacrifices made to save up for this
extraordinary and costly item that I was sure
she would enjoy. Ok, so I was wrong. And the
fact that I borrow it quite often should not
erase the thought behind the gift. I try.

Things changed when I met Guy.

It was a cool spring night when I stopped at
Clancy's to fortify my spirits after a painfully
exhausting day at the office copy machine. I
plopped down and ordered my usual ginger ale
when a burly chap sat next to me. His
expression could best be described as resembling
a person who just found out his wallet is
missing, worse yet, one who had left it in the
glove box of his truck which is also missing.

He told Clancy to give him a double of the
strongest stuff on the shelf; said he had a
fishing trip planned with the church and his
partner came down with the flu and unless he
could find another fisherman he'd have to call
off the trip.

I "Ah hummmmed" loud enough to shatter a
beer mug on a table thirty feet away and judging
by the eyes that narrowed to slits and the
clenched teeth, the fellow beside me may have
noticed. He swivelled in my direction and I
offered my services as I had quite innocently
overheard his predicament, and never one to pass
up a fishing trip. Only I had no idea what I
was getting in for.

He introduced himself as Guy and "the trip"
was an outing by which we would take nine deaf-
mute youngsters fishing to Mud Pond.

"Oh," I replied.

However I'd have a good deed to bring home
to the wife, proving without a doubt I'm not as
selfish as she declares, if I went through with

it. This might just put this silly notion of my
being selfish to rest once and for all.

So home I went and told my lovely spouse
about Guy.

She boomed, "You're always meeting a guy at
Clancy's! How much is it gonna cost this time?
A trip to Alaska? No wait, he sells trout
magnets right? Or maybe he has discount fly
rods made of alfalfa shoots?"

I retorted maturely, "No, smarty pants, not
a *guy*, his *name* is Guy and I'm going to do a
good deed; an unselfish act on my part!" (I
avoided saying, "Nyaa nyaa nyaa nyaa", in my
mature retort.)

I outlined the plan as Guy had laid it out
including the part where the youngsters
communicate with a language based on hand
signals and that they do not consider themselves
as handicapped. I was instructed not to treat
them as such either.

I thought I saw a twitch of understanding,
as at the end of my explanation my loyal,
understanding lady looked like she finally
realized how she had misjudged me. But looks
can be deceiving and she returned, "Oh? What's
the bottom line? They're all eighteen year old,
bleach-blonde bombshells? Or is Guy paying you
money I'll never see and you'll spend on a new
fishing stick from Orvis? If that's it, just
remember how I have to paint the kid's feet grey
so no one will notice the holes in their
sneakers."

So trusting, my wife. I felt it superfluous
at that point to mention that only five or six
of the group were eighteen year old young ladies
and certainly, while I did ascertain they were
blonde, whether they were bleached or not I
couldn't say. But surely the thought of payment
was beyond even her unwarranted cynicism.

Besides, Guy said, "No dice", to my casual
mention of informal guide fees.

Guy had a minibus from the church and off we
went; Guy, myself and nine of the nicest looking
kids you could find. They were well behaved
and, with sign language, Guy could converse with
them quite well as they with each other. They
all had fishing gear in one form or another and
as the bus rumbled along the kids appeared to be
having a good time. It was a bit spooky as it
was quiet as a cave whereas every bus trip I
took before was like the chimp cage at the zoo.

Then for a while all the kids were making
signs at once and Guy glanced in the rearview
mirror, stopped the bus and stood up.   He
shouted, "Knock it off!", and made a few hand
signals that were bordering on violent. His
face was red as he re-took the driver's seat and
we moved on. I was startled but whatever he
flashed at them with his big meaty hands did the
job. The kids sat motionless. I'll have to
learn that trick for the next family trip in the
station wagon.

I had been relegated to remove the knots
from the kids' lines, my having great experience
with backlash even to the extent of producing
Olympic quality tangles. I was thus engaged
when I looked up and saw the kids were once
again animated together. The bus stopped once
more and Guy repeated his performance of the
last stop.

We arrived shortly thereafter at Mud Pond
and the fishing began. Guy caught one lovely
fish and most of the youngsters caught at least
one keeper. I, on the other hand, maintained my
near perfect record of being skunked no matter
what the odds. I did, however, get to practice
once more, the removal of a barbed hook from my
fishing hat. I also made a spectacular cast to

a weedy patch of the pond which placed my
fishing hat squarely in the center. This seemed
to cheer the kids up some but having run out of
hats I was unable to duplicate the feat for
those who might have missed the technique.

Late afternoon arrived and the gang of boys
and girls got together, set their gear on the
ground and began motioning wildly as they had
before in the bus. With that, Guy burst through
the brush and began executing that intricate set
of hand motions and the kids became motionless.

Perplexed, (I had thought the day a great
success), I asked Guy, who stood holding his
fishing rod with drops of Mud Pond slowly
bouncing off his boots, "What's up?"

He replied, "If I told 'em once, I told 'em
a thousand times, NO SINGING while I'm fishing
or driving the bus!"

My Daddy used sign language too. He would
point with the index finger of the right hand
and we'd meet behind the barn without a word
said.

CHAPTER 8

THIN ICE

It was Sunday and my two boys and I were sitting ritually around the t.v. waiting for the football marathon to start when the conversation turned to physical fitness. We all agreed you would have to be in pretty fair shape to play the game of football even though the odds were you wouldn't stay that way after playing it for a while. What we did not agree on was who was in better shape, the old man who professes to handle fishing, hiking, hunting and all sorts of other outdoor activities with relative ease, thank you very much, or those two young upstarts who both play hockey in regular leagues. I assured them that a little skating in shifts of a few minutes couldn't match the rigors of climbing Shatterack Mountain during big game season or trudging through the marsh on a goose hunt with the wind howling and ice forming on your tonsils.

The argument continued through the whole first half and a ham and Swiss sandwich apiece, a bowl of greasy chips, a bag of tacos with bacon flavored salsa, two giant Cokes each and an eight ounce sack of cheese puff balls.

Recognition of our mutual crime set in almost
simultaneously and we pushed aside the empty
bowl, plates and tumblers; evidence if you wish.
I could lose a few pounds in a week or so if I
wanted too; no problem. The boys, not yet
overweight, with the metabolism of youth still
in full swing, were, however, not being kind to
their physique with all the consumed fats and
sugars. Boy! things were much more fun before
they invented cholesterol.

In any event the argument was not settled by
the end of the game which lead to the challenge.
We decided to have a "skate out". The first one
to quit skating looses. I used to skate right
well years ago but I haven't put the things on
in many, many moons. How I ever let myself get
talked into this I'll never know. But it was
two against one. So what, I suspect its like
riding a bike; you never forget.

We got up to our little cabin in the woods,
which is blessed with a pond that has no choice
but to freeze during the winter, only to find
eight inches of new fallen snow covering the
ground. It also covered the pond. It took most
of the morning to shovel, push, sweep and cajole
the tons of snow from the surface off to the
sides. Buy mutual agreement the "skate off"
would begin after lunch; well after lunch.

Meanwhile I was dusting off my old Bauers;
the skates that could have launched me into a
famous hockey career. If only I was a little
bigger, a little faster, knew a bit more about
hockey, had some talent, and if I wasn't offered
a great job in the shipping department of a
local manufacturer that paid cash money.

I was accused of procrastination but
actually my laces, not being used
in...well...quite some time, were pretty rotten
and broke in a number of places; honest. This

required a search for new laces (this takes
time), re-lacing (this also takes time), and
finally strapping the things on my feet. I'll
admit I didn't rush the procedure as I dwelled
some on the sanity of the upcoming event. This
was not made any easier by the taunting from the
young tigers lacing their own skates up. When I
explained that the laces were old; the boys
mentioned the laces were not the only thing that
was old rekindling the argument.

The boys declared the contest officially
under way as they finished with their skates and
headed for the pond. Oh! what a deepened hole
we dig with the shovel of pride.

Eventually it was time to stand up; the
moment of truth. Yes, you can forget how to
ride a bike. Memories of skating seasons long
ago rapidly slid from view and the here and now
was, in fact, here and now. That didn't make it
any easier. I kind of duck walked to the pond
and the show began.

I realized I was in a world of trouble, on
thin ice, so to speak, and had possibly allowed
myself to be taken in. Undaunted I set out with
a perfect stride. "Form is everything," I was
once coached by one of my hockey mentors and my
form as I fell on my duff was beyond reproach.
However, in no time at all I was going fine;
straight ahead that is. Turning was the next
thing I had to re-master and all I can say is
I'm thankful snow is soft. I dotted the edge of
the pond where we had piled the snow, with man-
like impressions until I began to get the hang
of it again and I commenced to turn and twirl
with something akin to my former grace. My
gracefulness had once been likened to that
delicate bird they call the elephant.

Next on the agenda was stopping. There are
several methods used today including the one I

used first; the forward-arm-waving-spread-eagle-
coast. Then I tried the backward-keester-
bumping-heel drag and finally the hockey stop
which the boys were generous enough to
demonstrate just inches from my prostrate form,
spraying chipped ice all over me which would
have gone very nicely in a martini with some
vodka, vermouth and a twist, thank you. Soon,
though, I was skating rather nicely, just a
shadow of my former genius, you understand, but
nicely. 'Round and 'round we went, lap after
lap. We raced end for end, time after time.
Visions of small green oxygen cylinders danced
in my head. And I don't want to say it was cold
or anything but as we exchanged good natured
jibes, I noticed the words froze. This became
tricky; skating over piles of shattered words.
For safety I stopped the good natured jibes,
that and the fact that I couldn't breathe and
jibe good naturedly at the same time. It was
shut up or stop skating and sit on a nearby rock
and jibe away. The latter choice was not
permitted by the dastardly duo; they weren't
through with me yet.

My number one son asked if my skates were
sharpened. My memory, apparently not improving
with time, had let me down. I meant to get them
sharpened but forgot. Therefore, I naturally
answered, "Of course." I meant they were
sharpened roughly around the time they
discovered penicillin, but yes, they had been
sharpened.

But oddly enough I wasn't doing too badly.
The mystery dissolved when I realized we were
skating on pond ice. Pond ice, by the way, is
not the same as rink ice and that's where I had
the unmistakable edge, no pun intended. My two
scoundrels had spent their entire skating
careers on nicely groomed rink ice; smooth as a

baby's heel. I, on the other hand, have
virtually never tasted such luxury. My youthful
years were spent scurrying after pucks on Mill
Pond and Twin Lakes. I was totally familiar
with the teeth-chattering, bone-jarring
washboard effect you often get on pond ice.
This at least kept me in the game for a while.

Then there was the crowd. The natives had
gathered to watch the Kids vs. the Old Geezer
contest. I could tell they smelled blood. It
was clear they were not rooting for the Old
Geezer. Their tormenting jeers were
unnecessary, as were the snowballs apparently
directed at the Old Geezer. Very funny. Thank
goodness their aim was no better than my skating
but the erratic skating method I was performing
by then made a remarkably difficult target.
This was all actually overkill anyway. The
results were already fait accompli, as they say.

Eventually the kids won and I was forced to
admit the old man wasn't in quite the shape I
wished. My legs ached, the feet were numb and
another area was sore beyond belief. There was
a significant dent in my pride as well. There's
a lot to be said for youth (but don't totally
discount old age and treachery).

Later the boys were laughing merrily over
the whole affair. As I laughed right along
with them it was a masterful deceit as I
suppressed tears of pain. My knees were
screaming, "How could you do this to us?" My
back had a similar query. I hoped I could keep
up the facade long enough for the boys to decide
it was time to turn in. Then I could crawl
under my own covers and let out the pent up
howl. Even in defeat pride gives up not easily.

My Daddy used to say, "You're only as old as
you feel...the next day!"

CHAPTER 9

I 'DRUTHER BE A COWBOY

Whoever first coined the "Peter Principle"
sure knew what he was talking about. That's
where the better you are at something the more
likely you are to be promoted until finally
you're in a position at which you are totally
inept and you're no longer promoted; works just
like that.

I considered myself very good at my job and
so eventually was promoted and swiftly promoted
again. Now I watch folks do what I enjoyed and
offer sage advice and tired wisdom every now and
then while I bury myself in paperwork.

All I ever really asked out of life was a
break. Like maybe Orvis would be looking for a
highly paid rod tester or perhaps Winchester
would need an at-large reporter to follow their
products in the field. But, no, instead I put
little pieces of information carefully within
the confines of small boxes outlined in light
green all the better for the computer you know!

Since my childhood, which only just ended,
my favorites have always been cowboys. No
little green boxes for those guys! Hopalong
Cassidy, Roy Rogers (and I'm not prejudiced, but

Dale Evans is certainly no cow*boy*), Randolph
Scot, et al., were my heroes. I mean they were
always out there riding the range on horses with
clever names where the fishin' and huntin' was.
They were never more than a stone's throw away
from a trap line, let alone other excitement
like Injuns and bad guys in black hats.

Well recently on a typical interesting
Friday afternoon at work I had the office door
closed and had propped my feet up on the desk
really getting into the little green box
stuffing routine when I decided to check my
eyelids for leaks.

I decided to chuck all the fame I've gotten
with the little greenies and be a cowboy. As I
left the office I paused just long enough to
dump a stack of those irritating forms with the
boxes, in the trash. I chose to take with me
only the essentials. Cowboys were never real
fussy guys so I took only those necessities like
a few changes of clothes, bed roll, fly rod and
reel, my trusty thirty-thirty and some ammo (for
some reason, though, the cowboys in the movies
never ran out and never reloaded), some beef
jerky in case I got stuck away from camp for a
few hours, and my Sony Walkman. The trip was
long and arduous but I arrived in time for chow
on a cloudless night on the range and I thought,
"Gee, this is gonna' be great bein' a cowboy and
all."

Chow turned out to be beef jerky and beans
which I considered ironic, ha ha. I asked where
a feller could find some good fly fishin' in the
area. "No time fer fly fishin', pardner," I was
told. There was clean up of camp, mending the
reins, bending the irons, some nasty jobs
concerning the horses, to which the whole world
is a toilet, and other stuff. "We're up at four
in the morning," someone mumbled. This caused

me a little surprise since I believed there was
a blank between midnight and seven.

And sure enough we were up before dawn and I
noticed my own scrawny legs dangling out of my
bed roll. I tugged on a pair of cowboy boots
and popped on my cowboy hat. Breakfast was beef
jerky and left over beans. This probably
accounted for the strange perfume in the air.
But I'm a cowboy; nothing's too tough for me.

We pushed cows all day like cowboys are
supposed to and around about noon we broke for
lunch in the field. Yep, beans an' jerky which
I took a pass on this time and thought I'd just
get in a little fishing while my "pardners"
hopefully finished the beans. However, we were
apparently in a hurry to get those cows
somewhere else so there was no time. The cows,
on the other hand, seemed indifferent as to
schedule.

Sometime after dark we arrived at a trifle
more civilized place and I was told to head for
the "bunkhouse". Hoo boy! I couldn't wait.
I've dreamed of the "bunkhouse" for years; what
with homey atmosphere, little potbelly stove,
card games going on, great chats about cowboy
stuff and lots of good natured joshing among the
hands. There would be guys with names like
Shorty and Big Jim; it was going to be all I
expected. But then I was told we were a bit
late and the boss was furious. The boss? Lord
love a duck, we had a *boss*? My suggestion that
we use the microwave to save some time was met
with a round of cowboy laughter and, you guessed
it, the cook brought the jerky and beans for a
quick supper. This leant a gamey aroma to the
bunkhouse making it much like the camp we left.

I was pretty whipped after chow and figured
to climb into the old bunkbed and said so to a

few of the other cowhands. They informed me,
"Not just yet. Ya' gotta fill out the forms."

One dude with grey hair spilling out from
under his Stetson said, "Yeah; gotta report on
the day's progress on the range."

Another injected, "Get a bunch of those
forms over there, the ones with the little green
boxes. And stay within the green boxes for
heavens sake or ya' gotta start all over again.
The computer ya' know."

At that exact moment the "boss" opened the
bunkhouse door. And darned if it didn't look
just like Roy Rogers!

Simultaneously, as I've had happen in dreams
before, Roy was replaced by Mr. Armstrong my
real boss standing in the doorway. My feet
fairly bounced to the floor and my chair sprung
upright. He calmly inquired where my suppose-
to-be-finished stack of forms with the little
green boxes were. I started to tell him they
were back at the bunkhouse but thought better of
it; the sneer building on his face left little
doubt that was not such a hot idea.

Even in a daydream I never did get to go
fishing. At least with the crumby job I've got
now I get to go on weekends so I guess I'll just
save the cowboys for heroes and stay right here
filling in the tiny green boxes.

My Daddy used to say, "The devil you know is
often better than the one you don't."

CHAPTER 10

HAVE A MICE DAY

A good friend of mine, Merathaim Johnson, (his folks were apparently bible conscious) related the following outlandish tale. Some say my pal, Merry, is a half-bubble off plumb but I don't believe it. I don't swear that the tale is true either 'cause I wasn't there; I will, however, attest that he was indeed sober at the time of telling, if not necessarily at the time of its alleged occurrence.

Merry owns a small cabin on the edge of Lake St. Catherine, in Vermont, and is about the prettiest spot on earth. Mer is an avid fisherman and sometime hunter. The camp offered superb opportunities for his fishing activities during the warmer months, as I have, on several occasions, joined him and had a splendid time. He did not, though, use it during late fall and winter because the whole area is deserted after Labor Day. Well last year he decided that even though the place was not really equipped for year-round use it did have a small fireplace and might afford a quiet little haven for a hunter as there are many acres around on state land for hunting.   Thus he approached the camp the day

before hunting season opened and shoveled the
meager two inches of snow until he gained the
front door. It really must have looked
beautiful with new fallen snow dressing it up.

     After getting a nice blaze crackling in the
fireplace, Merry then prepared his guns and gear
for use first thing in the morning. The fire
died down and he unrolled his sleeping bag and
adjusted things, with a smile of anticipation
attached, for a good night's sleep.

     Now anyone who's had the pleasure, knows
that there's simply nothing quieter than a
small, primitive cabin in the woods covered with
a blanket of snow on a cold, windless night. In
fact you'd have to die to get less noise. No
electric gadgets whirring, no dripping,
pressurized faucets; no nothing
Er...well...except for the mouse.

     Merry was not at all accustomed to mice as
they never seemed to bother entering the cabin
in the summer, but, again, anyone who has been
interrupted in sleep by La Mouse knows that the
noise one can make gnawing, for instance, on the
edge of a plastic garbage can will sound about
the same as the excavation for the Verazano
Narrows Bridge.

     Crunch!...Crunch!...Snap!...Crunch! Quickly
a flashlight beam shattered the blackness and
silence was once again restored. Nothing in
sight. Flashlight off.
Crunch!...Crunch!...Snap!...Crunch! Flashlight
on; silence. After a few rounds of this
entertaining game Mer leaped out of his sleeping
bag and, poised at a crouch in his skivvies,
held the loaded flashlight at the ready in the
dark.

     One should realize at this point that a
cabin is wonderfully cozy when one is sitting in
front of the blazing fireplace, legs crossed, a

warming Scotch whiskey in hand waiting for
memories to knock and beg to be let out.
However,...and I caution you not to accuse
exaggeration...once that fine, radiating flame
is extinguished the temperature in the cabin
will plummet at a rate rivaling the dive of the
great red hawk.

So with legs turning blue and chattering
knees and teeth now disturbing the blessed
stillness themselves, my friend listened and at
the first "crunch', snapped on the light. The
first shot was wide of the mark but it did
disclose a very startled mouse who disappeared
into a small hole in the molding near the floor,
sort of Tom & Jerry-like. The noise quickly
returned after the light was shut off and as he
pulled the trigger on the flash again the mouse
disappeared once more. That's when Mer ran out
of ammo, so to speak, and the flashlight
failed; slowly dying down until not even a glow
was left as a reminder of the once brilliant
weapon.

Reaching for what he thought was a wad of
paper kept ready to kindle the fire, my buddy
stuffed same into the hole in the molding. It
worked! After a short defrost period he slept
through the night.

It was the next morning, early as you would
imagine, Merry awakened and jumped into his
hunting togs. He stuffed his pockets with keys,
pocket watch, small change, knife, and his roll
of...where was that roll of bills he brought to
buy victuals at the general store, a brewskie or
two and gas for the truck to get home. The
puzzle was answered when he spied a minute pile
of confetti near the mouse hole, including
partial pictures of Alexander Hamilton and
George Washington.

My Daddy used to say, "Don't put your money where your mouse is!"

CHAPTER 11

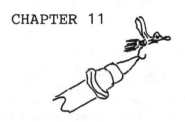

FLY FISHIN' SURE GETS IN YOUR BLOOD

It was rather accidental, our meeting; me
and Fred Deschler. If it had not been for my
propensity to be klutzy and he being inclined
somewhat in the same direction we probably never
would have met.

I was attending one of those parties one
must endure when one is married and one's spouse
insists that one should go regardless of whether
one agrees or not. Normally I would just say,
"Phooey" and head for the basement to tie some
flies but this time she had turned on the
waterworks and pulled all stops so I really had
to go.

This particular gathering required, get
this, a suit and tie of all things; not my kind
of party. And owning only one suit, I was bound
and determined to protect it no matter what. I
sidestepped everyone with a drink in their hand,
ducked the hors d'oeuvre trays, passed up the
buffet and generally tried to stay centered and
on my guard. And if this wasn't enough of a
drag I couldn't even find a cold beer in the
place. All they had were drinks with stupid
names and stuff floating in them.

I was doing real well until I met Fred.

Very, very cautiously I was backing away
from an overstuffed lady who was precariously
waving something in a glass I suspected to be
stronger and more staining than ginger ale, with
one hand, and what appeared to be a tiny hot dog
in a napkin with *mustard* on it with the other,
when I was brought up short by someone bumping
into me from the back. As I turned around to
meet Fred for the first time we both heard the
unmistakable sound of a fabric at full rip. It
happened that Fred was backing carefully away
from a banker with an ominously glowing cigar,
protecting *his* only suit! The rip, it was
discovered, thank goodness, was a throw rug of
some neat Persian looking material that
succumbed during the collision, and not either
of our precious suits.

We both wore sheepish grins as the hostess
approached. Between us we figured we could
raise a mortgage enough to pay for the thing.
For several deafening minutes all conversation
had stopped and all eyes were turned in our
direction as we were about to get a verbal
thrashing. But, as luck would have it, she
merely said, "It's nothing, I'm throwing it out
anyway."

Well Fred and I both dropped to our knees
and inspected the furry piece, each recognizing
the look of insanity found in avid fly tyers
pouncing on new material. Fred indicated it
might just make a decent Hendrickson. I, on the
other hand, thought more like a Dark Cahill.
Seeing as how she was discarding it anyhow we
finished the job of tearing it in half; half for
Fred and half for me. The looks on the faces of
the crowd as the conversation slowly geared back
up told me for sure these folks didn't
understand a fly tyer.

So that's how Fred and I got acquainted.
Both our suits suffered from kneeling on the
floor but the good news was we didn't have to
guard them after that and proceeded to dig into
the onion dip and potato salad. Our friendship
continued for quite some time until Fred got a
real job and moved to New Jersey.

In our day, Fred and I fished many miles of
the Battenkill, the Beaverkill, the Delaware and
lot's of local areas with no names. We had a
rare fellowship and I missed him aplenty when he
left for Jersey.

Fred fell on hard times in New Jersey, it
turned out. First his wife left him claiming
she could stand not one more minute with a man
whose greatest thrill is tying replicas of dead
bugs. Then his new home burned to the ground.
I mean they say there was nothing left but ash;
a short circuit somewhere they later said. Then
after losing his job he took up logging in
upstate New York and in an accident with a saw,
lost two fingers on his right hand.

I, of course, did not know all this when I
next met Fred. He had stopped in at a game
supper at a church upstate. I happened to be
there and spotted him across the big room. I
practically ran over and yelled, as folks often
do, "How's it goin' Freddie old boy?"

He hung his head and from the look on his
face I realized something was desperately wrong.
I then wished I hadn't been so exuberant.

Fred really looked down when he replied,
"Not so good Al my friend. Only got two browns
this morning; something wrong with my Blue Dun's
I think!"

My Daddy used to say, "The Lord put limits
on man's wisdom but none on his stupidity."

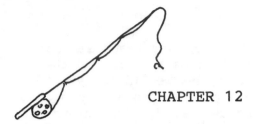

CHAPTER 12

MULES AND FOOLS

There's a reason these two words rhyme. And
I'm convinced I now know why. Make me a
promise; if you start to read this, read the
whole thing. Once you begin you're committed,
okay?

The story began like this:

At the Great Sportsmen's Expo show, I was
happily engaged at our club booth chatting with
some fine folks about fly fishing, selling
raffle tickets and generally having a good time
trying to solicit membership. In any case,
directly across from our tiny spot in the show
was a fellow by the name of A. J. Wanamaker
representing his "Mountain Adventures On Mules".
And of course, keeping him company, was Monday,
a mule of no insignificant size.

There would, on occasion, come a time when
Monday would yield to the call of nature, mules
not being in the least bit modest, and the crowd
would thin out perceptibly for a while in our
little corner of the building. This gave us
plenty of time to talk to A. J. about his
adventures on mules. Well to shorten a lengthy
tale, our club booked a trip to do some fly

fishing on some unspoiled, wilderness streams in
Pennsylvania approachable only on muleback.
This was the first such trip the club
arranged...therefore we can be forgiven I guess.

I spent four anxious months dreaming of
standing in big, wild water in my L.L. Bean
waders tossing fifty foot casts to huge trout;
playing leaping fish time after time.

The big day finally came and our group of
five from the club set off in high spirits
swapping lies about previous trips and proudly
displaying our collections of hand tied flies.
In one car were Morty and Herb and in Joe's
shiny new van were Joe, Mike and Yours Truly.
We braved Friday afternoon traffic and
eventually arrived in Jim Thorpe, PA, where fun
was being stored up just for us.

When we pulled up to the door of the
"Mountain Adventures On Mules" headquarters it
looked very much like an abandoned Waldbaum's
Supermarket, all concrete block and cement. We
were greeted by Joan Snurdly, chief
receptionist, cook, arranger and all around get-
it-doner. There was good hearted joshing with
Joan and our soon-to-be-guide-for-the-second-
day, Dan Chancy (a fine name for a guide). We
were shown the "lounge", a homey collection of
wooden picnic tables and comfortably tattered
chairs and, thank goodness, a perpetual coffee
pot. So we didn't book the Holiday Inn...right?
Next stop, the "bunkhouse". I still have a dent
in my chest where my jaw bounced as we were lead
through a man-made tunnel to eight by ten rooms
with two cots and a 25 watt light bulb. We only
spend a few hours in there sleeping
anyway...correct? We still wore smiles,
however, as visions of that big water and
leaping fish ran through our heads.

Joan explained at dinner (Meatloaf Surprise which was simply delicious!) that we were breaking tradition, "Heh, heh, heh," and would be taken by truck to the start of our adventure and would work our way up Hell's Creek to where the mules would await our arrival willing and capable of bringing us back (to Waldbaum's) in style. We would be pioneers, "Heh, heh, heh," and try a new scheme where two of us would fish one stream and the other three a second stream which join as Hell's Creek. We would dine for lunch at the fire road at which point our guide for the day, Cathy Snurdly, go figure, would meet us with the fixin's.

That evening we had some great good fun trading jibes with a bunch of turkey hunters finishing a few days afield at their sport and we wisecracked with a gang of fishermen planning to use "garden hackle" or wo...wor...wor...sorry, just can't say it. There was even some lighthearted talk about bears and rattlesnakes we might meet on the trail, "Heh, heh, heh." Then we were off to the "bunkhouse" after a few beers and a good quantity of laughs.

As the truck slithered to a stop in the mud at 7:30 A.M., Joan casually suggested to our disembarking group that we divide up between this stream and the one we just passed. "What *stream we just passed*?", my mind screamed out. I've had bigger faucet leaks than the *stream we just passed*. "What's wrong with this picture?" my inner me asked as I stood next to a squirt of water three feet wide and barely six inches deep, in chest waders adorned with corkers and holding on to an 8 and 1/2 foot fly rod. It may have looked rather ridiculous (I certainly *felt* ridiculous) but, indeed, this was the tag end of Hell's Creek we were to fish.

My first thought was, "You can't cast here
in this overgrown Garden of Eden!"
   Beautiful it was, but my intuition was
correct; there was simply no way to cast a fly.
We were reduced to dapping a fly at the end of,
maybe, six foot of exposed leader. I sure hope
no one took any pictures. I was beginning to
understand why the "garden hackle" guys made out
so well; all you'd need is a stick and a string
like I used forty years ago at Browning's Lake
in my home town, which incidentally, now has a
school on it.
   Joe raised our spirits immensely when he
speculated that things would surely get better
at the point where the two streams joined
forces. Unfortunately the difference was almost
imperceptible as we reached the spot where the
two trickles became one slightly larger trickle.
   By 10:30 we had tested and surpassed the
established limits of frustration. We had not
seen, much less caught, a fish. I, personally,
logged approximately 50% of my fishing time re-
tying flies, plucking same from trees, replacing
tippets and extracting hooks from weeds, rocks
and my hat! Mike developed a method he calls
his "bow and arrow" cast. The sequence goes
like this: step one, you grab the fly between
the thumb and forefinger with about six our
seven feet of leader out; step two, holding the
line fast with the other hand, pull back and
load the rod and release; step three, remove
hook from thumb or index finger and repeat step
one. Thanks Mike.
   While we were enjoying all this it became
evident that we were steadily climbing. In fact
between us and the mules which would swiftly and
delicately put an end to this fly fisherman's
nightmare, was a mountain. It is still nameless
in my notebook but *there* never-the-son-of-a-gun-

less! We were now engaged in mountain climbing
wearing chest waders, working our way over
rocks, dense briars and killer rhododendrons
waving and 8 and one half foot fly rod. Perhaps
there's a more uncomfortable way to climb a
mountain but I've yet to hear of it.

Well somewhere during the agony we began to
catch fish. The first to be caught, let the
records show or I'm in big trouble, was by Mike.
So what if it looked suspiciously like a minnow,
it was a fish. As fish began to show up things
brightened and after some five hours we overtook
the fire road and there was Cathy, our guide,
looking cool and calm after schlepping a pack
that weighed marginally less than she; full of
great sandwiches, iced tea, fruit and a load of
other gear. She said it took her an hour to get
down from where the mules were so we should take
our time; after all we had all day, "Heh, heh,
heh." Climbing down and climbing *up* are
entirely two different endeavors.

We fished miniature pool after miniature
pool taking fish now and again but more often
retrieving flies from trees. I don't want to
say that Mike ran ahead to get the best pools
first so I won't say it. He did, however, get
the most fish for the day; eleven. Mike,
somewhat bashful about his accomplishment, would
mention it no more than three or four times in
the course of subsequent conversations. And I'm
positive about the number 'cause I found it
carved into my tackle box, rod case and waders.
Morty and Herb got their fair share too. Joe
and I lagged somewhat behind having a hard time
erasing those visions of big water, leaping
trout. Actually my best catch was Herb's hat
which floated down stream to where I was fishing
and being a size 7 and 7/8, I believe it

qualifies for the record catch of the day.
Others disagree.

So up, up, up we went wading the stream and
sometimes climbing the trail until my ancient
watch told me it was 5 P.M. We had put in three
hours since lunch and, gee, the mules had to be
just around the next bend, right?? Wrong.

We now gave up even the pretense of fly
fishing, collapsed the rods and stuffed the
reels in our pockets just to get through the
cutthroat rhododendron. It was pure survival
now. Then, God bless her, there was Cathy
waving a big "Howdy". Could the mules be far
behind? You bet.

Cathy, sweet as she was, had double barreled
bad news for us. First she said, "You're
halfway there." *Halfway there*! *Halfway there*!
Our hearts skipped a few collective beats.
Halfway there!

Secondly she said, "The mules are there,"
pointing to the top of yet another mountain. I
apologize publicly for my thoughts at that
particular moment.

But we all got there somehow and slipped
into the mule saddles which were very
comfortable; considering. By then we were numb
and it was 7:30 P.M. with a two hour trek yet to
go to the "bunkhouse". We were wet, cold, tired
beyond comprehension and hungry. And...there
was a whole new dimension added to our fun; it
was getting dark. Now we were to duck branches,
etc., in the dark on muleback. There are few
things less pleasant than a poke in the eye with
a stick.

We arrived at 9:30 to a hot meal, cold beer
and another round of the comraderie that made
the trip worthwhile.

Next morning we set out on our second day to
fish Stony Creek. The water was bigger and

wilder but we all got skunked. Dan, our guide
for the day, and sensible precautions, prevented
a re-run of the first day. However, we did
catch fish the previous day regardless of the
trials. Hmmmm...maybe we should go back?

I'd go again.

My Daddy used to say, "Sometimes a fly
fisherman can be as stubborn as a ....!"

CHAPTER 13

THERE'S A LEEK IN MY PANCHO

This tale is dedicated to Mike Murray, my fishing and hunting pal since...well, let's see, it was just after they discovered gravity. Mike is an avid fisherman and hunter. However, it has been on a number of long trips to far off fishing haunts that I was exposed to his real talents. After logging hundreds of suffering hours listening to his seemingly endless collection of the worst puns, oxymorons, equivokes and other corruptions of what we used to call language, prior to Mike's total disassembly, my head lolled from side to side like a football player who has had too many downs without a helmet. I've decided Mike is the king of such matters. On the q.t. his lovely wife confided that she is not hard of hearing as Mike believes but rather has the special gift of selective listening.

But king though he may be, let it not be without competition and in this literary tome, I will attempt to do better...or worse if you like. Anyway, Mike, "This butts for you!"

(Note: I'll put these little quotations marks in so you'll recognize the funny parts. o.k.?).

Well it seems that two friends of mine, Ralph Armstrong and Roy Stone had gotten a little bored with the usual whitetail big game hunt and decided to save a few bucks (no pun intended, I haven't started yet; that one's free), and go to Mexico to hunt wild boar and javelina. Things went well at first but as they travelled no-name roads on foot in search of the camp the newspaper ads called *Javelina Heaven* they got somehow turned around and disoriented. As they wandered through the damp mountains they came on a tiny cabin in the woods which was empty and seemed a great place to rest and think things over. Roy stumbled across the portal and banged his elbow on a nail protruding from the door but there was very little in the way of injury as "you can't get blood from a Stone" (We're rolling now).

The cabin was bare but had a small supply of spicy canned food and a whole bunch of tennis equipment. There was also a box hidden in a secret compartment containing only some kind of animal call manufactured by H & H Mooney and a weathered looking compass by the Tates Company. The owners of the cabin were not worried; "nobody takes cache anymore". They set their stuff down and began to relax. Roy, always mindful of his possessions, cleaned off his brand, spanking new boots and set them outside the door to dry. At about this same time two Mexicans were bicycling on up the road; they had been out gathering materials from paper birch trees with which to build a canoe. The first Mexican, whose name turned out to be Pancho, was burdened heavily with the canoe fixin's and also their vittles which was mostly wild onions. He found it difficult to steer, what with all the

paper birch stuff he had collected, and crashed
into the side of the camp. You might say "his
bark was bigger than his bike" (wait, wait,
we're just warming up). In the resulting tumble
the wild onions became deeply jammed in his
pockets and indeed there were several "leeks in
our Pancho" (now we get serious).

At the sound of the commotion Roy and Ralph
quickly looked around and grabbed the first
thing at hand from the tennis stuff, their guns
having been stowed, and stood at the ready.
When Pancho threw open the door and saw our boys
standing there all he could say was, "You boys
sure make quite a racket!"

They all grinned and Pancho introduced
himself and his companion Juan. Roy and Ralph
spelled out their predicament and were informed
that there were neither wild boar (there was,
however, wild bore), nor javelina for thousands
of miles. There were, though, some very large
and dangerous animals called cad in the region.
Pancho explained that cad live mainly in holes
in the cliffs called leids. He further reported
that the cad were hunted by a local tribe whose
chieftain was called Ketch. The herd had
thinned out to the point that in the last few
years it's just been "catch as Ketch can". The
tribe, which lived on the very edge of the
mountain, an area known only as South Ear, were
reduced to making inexpensive ladies' pocket
books for trade. Even this didn't work out too
well 'cause everyone knows "you can't make a
silk purse out of the South Ear". But Pancho
insisted that he could still offer them a fine
hunt as he alone knew of a passage in the hills
and if they would hire himself and Juan they
would show Roy and Ralph the "leid at the end of
the tunnel". Pancho, nobody's fool, wanted a

contract though and they agreed to tackle it
first thing in the morning.

When they awoke, Roy's attention was drawn
to the cabin window where he saw some enormous
creature making off with his brand, spanking new
boots in its mouth. That was the end of his
fancy footwork, as it were.

Roy then set to the contract business and
was agreeable to all terms but wanted to know
why they would need both of them as guides.
Pancho replied that on a cad hunt he was the
business partner but in reality "it takes Juan
to know one". Ralph, unlike Roy, was adamantly
opposed to the contract and shunned the whole
procedure. But he softened under the persuasion
of both Pancho and Roy. Juan had gone outside
earlier for a breath of fresh air and now that
Ralph was ready to enter into the agreement
Pancho thought it was time for Juan to come back
inside while the bargain was completed, lacking
only Ralph's signature. He told Roy to call him
from the cabin door and "make Hey! while the
shun signs".

Pancho indicated he was rather relieved
because looking at their gear, especially the
beat up compass, he knew they were in trouble
for "he who has a Tates is lost". Ralph and Roy
asked how to get started with the hunt and Juan
picked up the animal call and instructed Ralph
to go to the front of the cabin and "put his
Mooney where his mouth is" and give a blow.
Doing this brought an almost immediate response
from the brush and a big, ugly animal charged
for the cabin door. As he slammed the door he
asked, "Pardon me Roy, is that the cad who
chewed your new shoes?" (you old timers will get
it; say it fast).

Roy allowed as how it might be. Pancho then
insisted that they build a fire to ward off an

attack but all they could find available was a
half-filled can of ancient kerosene. But then,
"there's no fuel like an old fuel", so they used
it. Soon they had a good blaze going.

At the sight, a wondrous thing occurred.
The cads began to line up in a single file like
they were waiting for the next available teller
at a bank. Juan claimed they were simply
forming lines but Pancho rebuffed him saying
they were actually columns. Ralph said it
really didn't matter, "a rows by any other name
is still..."

He never got a chance to finish as Roy
interrupted by whimpering loudly. He was told
because of that he would not get supper. Pancho
declared he would "serve no whine before it's
time".

The actual hunt was delayed a full day
because after the cads were driven away by the
fire the place was overrun by rabbits from the
surrounding bushes. There were rabbits just
everywhere underfoot but Pancho claimed it would
simply hold them up a day since they're "hare
today and gone tomorrow".

And soon it was time to take the bull by the
horns, so to speak, and Roy and Ralph began
putting on their hats and hunting clothes
readying for the hunt. Pancho criticized them
severely, reciting a local pearl that says,
"Don't suit until you see the whites of their
eyes." It was only minutes later that Ralph
dropped the lead cad buck with one shot.

This was an exciting trip, one which none of
us are likely to forget, although you may try.
Upon returning home with the mounted head, Ralph
ran into some, not so unexpected, resistance
from his wife about its placement on the den
wall, ugly as it was. She would compromise no
further than permitting it outside on top of the

metal shed. Now in summer it's, more or less, a
"cad on a hot tin roof".
     You win Mike, I just can't do it.
     My Daddy used to say, "It's fun to pun, but
when you're done the score is none..for
everyone."

CHAPTER 14

THE $1000 TRIP

October is the time of year when I'm
reminded of my first backpacking excursion.
It's a great season for a lot of outdoorsy stuff
'cause it's cool and the scent of fall in the
air adds a bit of excitement with winter
pending.

It was on a beautiful see-your-breath
morning that I trekked up Shatterack mountain on
a three day backpacking trip. Actually the trip
was uneventful and did not begin a long and
glorious career of backpacking for me as I'm
sure you thought I was about to say. The only
noteworthy thing about it, now that I recall,
mainly because my lovely spouse reminds me at
every opportunity, is its cost.

It began, in fact, with my reading an issue
of *Outdoor Life* magazine which did a rather
thorough treatise on the subject of backpacking.
In the vernacular of the law this should really
have been called entrapment since I never before
that article had contemplated storing an entire
home on my back to go schlepping up mountain
trails to spend the nights fostering arthritis
of the back on cold ground when I own, and pay a

steep mortgage on, a wonderful, heated home well
insulated from mosquitos, bats, and such.

But as I read on I could feel the wanderlust
building and soon every vein and artery was
screaming, "Let's go!" Had I snapped the
magazine shut at that point I might still have
been saved. Only I didn't. Instead I read
right on through the 'how to get started', the
'tips and suggestions', and the two pages of
required gear.

Shortly thereafter I combined my newly
acquired insanity with a life-long ambition; a
trip to Freeport, Maine and L.L. Bean's famous
outfitters shop. The expense of that trip has,
in fact, not even been factored into the costs
and it's a fair 350 mile shot from my home on
the Isle of Long in New York, requiring gas
stops, lunch and dinner stops not to mention the
fact that the rest of the family was also along
multiplying the cost at each of the stops.

L.L. Bean has been my favorite mail order
place since boyhood and a trip to the home store
has been a dream for thirty years and now I was
there. I was right there; the birthplace of
most of my sporting equipment! I like L.L.'s
preference for goods made in the U.S. of A. and
a policy of quality first. Of course there's a
price tag attached to good stuff but I don't
know how many times I've bought cheap imitations
made offshore and ended up throwing it over for
the real thing eventually anyway.

Entering the store was practically a
religious experience for within those hallowed
confines was spawned hunting shirts, hats,
fishing rods, waders, fly tying tools, reels,
line, et al., that I've used for years and
years. And right smack in the middle of the
place, which is open to the public seven days a
week, 365 days a year, is a trout pond, for

goodness sake, harboring trout I'd be envious to
bring to the net any day!

After examining virtually every square inch
of the place I headed for serious consideration
to the "wilderness" section.

Here I obtained the lightweight, adjustable
frame, stain shedding, completely waterproofed
back pack into which I stuffed the following:
first aid kits, cook kits and snake bite kits.
We added backpacker's miniature, multi-fuel,
easy light stove, ultralight, wrinkle free, non-
rip, aluminum pole, self standing, one man,
three season tent, protrusion proof, moisture
resistant, insulated ground cloth, fold up, four
section, featherweight, super strong, fly
fishing rod with accessory case including micro
reel, line, and an assortment of classic flies,
a Fisherman's Pal and other sundries and fabrics
to match the hatch. And since no self
respecting backpacker would enter the woods in
the embarrassing collection of overweight, worn
out clothing I now use for hunting and fishing,
I purchased the all-weather, breathable, no
sweat shirt, the backpackers specially designed,
super soft shorts with matching, quick tug-on
hiking pants, gossamer, Gore-Tex, mid-height,
skid free, all new, trail boot, sun stopper,
adjustable band, ventilated yet 100% weather
rejecting backpackers hat and the roll-up, easy
store, watertight, nylon, unburdened jacket.
Then, of course, came the sleeping bag 'cause
the one I have for family camping weighs
slightly less than a Buick, the diminutive
camera, sunglasses, and, what else?, the freeze
dried gourmet foods into which you stir a small
quantity of water and perhaps add a little heat
and out pops a meal fit for a King; at least a
very hungry King (and backpacking tends to make
Kings like that).

As I say, the trip was relatively uneventful but it certainly still lives in my memory. The final tally was just about $1000 but the trip to L.L. Bean was worth it, accomplishing a lifelong goal. I'll be glad to let you know the date of the garage sale.

I've spoofed backpacking a bit but it really is great fun and wonderful exercise. You'll see a world you wouldn't even notice from a car, on a bike, or even just rushing along the trail to get somewhere. However, I do caution; *don't go it alone!* Nature still has some surprises left and they're not all pleasant. It's more fun with a few friends anyway.

My Daddy used to say, "If the Lord wanted us to be backpackers he'd have built a pocket in your skin", (waterproof, ultralight, non-wrinkle, anti-leak and self sealing).

CHAPTER 15

100% CHANCE OF RAIN

I was awakened by the ring of the phone. I
struggled awake to peer at my digital alarm
clock radio as my pupils did a spasm to focus
after having just been cozily resting behind
eyelids that now snapped open like faulty window
shades. It was four o'clock in the morning! I
slapped at the buttons to silence the silly
thing and in the attempt got tangled in its mane
of speaker wires, power cord and antenna,
finally realizing it was the cursed phone making
the racket.

I picked up the receiver and it promptly
said, "Hey, Al, Charlie and I are maybe goin'
fishin'; you got anything planned for today?"
This message came from my neighbor Ralph Gilles.

My mind was already about a light year ahead
of the conversation. Big Ralph and I have been
no more than casual friends since the third
grade but things do change don't they? I mean
maybe Ralph's not so bad after all. This
invitation, albeit at 4 A.M., might just be
evidence of an attempt to reconcile past
differences. And, then, some of the things that

have perhaps dampened a closer friendship might
just have been trivial folly. Like last winter
when Ralphie cut my rail fence in about twelve
places while whacking up some firewood with the
chainsaw in his yard. I guess this could happen
to anybody right? And the laughter was probably
just a nervous reaction to embarrassment.

I answered that I indeed had no plans for
the day. He then replied, "Great, then Charlie
and I are going fishing. See ya!" click. I'll
have to talk to him about that fence when they
get back.

I climbed back into bed and not twenty
minutes later the phone rang once more. Another
party of two wanting to know if I had any
outdoor plans for the day. My reputation is
apparently widespread and almost legendary.
It'd serve them right if I said, "Yeah, I'm
goin' fishin' *all day*, in a small boat and I'm
not even taking my slicker."

In fact many of my acquaintances have given
up altogether on other forms of weather
forecasts such as the newspapers, radio, t.v.,
or the National Weather Bureau. These sources
give you odds, like a "20% chance of rain." Or
sometimes even more ambiguous and complicated as
in; "There's a 20% chance of precipitation with
a 10% chance it will be snow and a likelihood of
1 to 3" accumulation if it does."

The severity of the storm is generally in
direct proportion to the importance of my plans.
There was an incident where I went a long
stretch on the job without any sort of vacation
whatsoever. So at the end of the stint I
decided the family would go camping for a week;
enjoy the great outdoors, as it were. It
happened that the country was locked in the grip
of a drought at the time. Upon our return we
were greeted by a large throng of appreciative

folks throwing wreaths and garlands as a tribute to my magic; having saved the crops of an entire nation. It felt good, actually.

Then there was the blizzard of '78. I had a grand hunting trip planned for that day.
And...oh...Hurricane Gloria; yep that was mine too..was supposed to fly to Canada for some late season fishing.

But no one invites me to go on trips anymore. I'm destined to plod on by myself. My family won't even allow me to participate in vacation plans. Dates and times are kept a secret until the very departure.

Well, got to go now. The phone is ringing again. This is the seventh call today; good thing for them I've got nothing planned.

My Daddy used to say, "Dawn has finally broken." And I used to say, "At least you can't blame me for that!"

CHAPTER 16

MEM'RIES

While cleaning out a seldom used closet, under the threat of divorce from my spouse of many years, I found the usual old collection of junk you save "just in case". This particular closet was the burial ground for much of my sporting goods which either outlived their expected useful life or were bonafide lemons to start out with. I had promised to shed our home of this blight for some three years but this year the very real prospect of violence had me tossing broken fishing reels, leaky boots (which I guarantee I could have fixed...someday), and other such valuable items in a carton destined to decorate the local dump.

I reached in the back and plucked from that dark corner, an old hunting jacket that even I would have to admit, with little coaxing, was worn beyond economical repair. A motion toward the infamous carton was halted in mid-toss by the fleeting notion to check the pockets. The last pocket inspected produced a tiny tin whistle, in itself worthless, with the plating worn off and adorned with dents and scratches.

The tiny whistle, extracted from a veritable
rag of a coat, which I had accused my wife of
throwing out years prior, had a special meaning.
The film reel in my mind rewound back some years
and stopped on a frame revealing a slightly
overweight Labrador retriever. The flickering
pictures in my head showed me standing by with
that little whistle in my hand while Tonky
cavorted across an open field. The whistle
belonged to he and I alone. Unorthodox, yes,
but then Tonky and I had no reason to worry
about it because the whistle worked and always
brought him back.

At the time maybe I figured Tonky to be a
brilliant bird dog. But being my first, I've
since learned the rascal was a comparative
dunce. No matter though, we shared an
understanding, man and dog, that couldn't be
recreated with best of breed, show, or field. I
recalled the many habits Tonky had, like his
penchant for resting not at my feet while I sat
and read a book in the evening, but *on* them; all
seventy pounds of him.

The frames skittered by and once again I
recalled how much I miss the old fellow. We
never got a whole lot of birds, he and I, but if
only he could be here again, to feel his big
head in my hand once more, he'd never have to
get one single bird.

The whistle brought back a treasured mem'ry
and I'm glad of it. No, the whistle didn't go
in the carton; never will. And if you won't
tell my adorable wife I'm truly happy she made
me clean that closet, well I won't either. I
suspect she guessed, though, when she spotted me
sitting on the floor with an old hunting jacket
on, a tear in my eye, and a toot on the badly
worn whistle calling, "Here Tonky, here Tonky."

Then there was the day a youngster in the
neighborhood, Michael by name, appeared in my
yard while I was inefficiently trying to fix the
shed door. He had in his hand a rather worn fly
rod which surely tasted many years streamside.
He wanted my opinion of it. And I said, as I'm
wont to do, "Dunno." I always say this when I'm
buying time lest my incurable ignorance become
even more public. He handed me the stick and
instantly I saw a rod identical to one I'd had
some decade and a half ago. The young
whippersnapper had rekindled another flame in my
mem'ry collection. I recalled the arguments
after its purchase amid a healthy stack of
unpaid bills which faced us newly weds. I
remembered that old green Berkley on which my
first day's catch was a single sunfish on an
extremely poorly tied (by me), Royal Coachman at
Mud Pond. Oh, and if you talk to the mother of
my kids, she'll tell you vividly how we divided
one sunfish for supper that evening. Her hero
had provided sustenance. The rod cast a little
better than an axe handle but I defended it
staunchly and we did manage to land a bunch of
fish eventually.
     The kid allowed me the time for my
flashback and then I pointed out the very
special, even superior features of this little
rod as I flailed it back and forth. The little
devil then said it was mine for ten bucks. This
was probably as much as I paid for my own
memorable version way back when. With a smile
I'm certain Michael never understood, I forked
over a ten spot.
     Not two days later Michael's grandfather
stopped by to make a trade; ten bucks for a
wonderful old green Berkley he'd had a long,
long time. Seems Michael found it in an old
closet leaning up against the wall, neglected,

in the dark for years, and obviously unneeded.
What he needed was ten bucks. The trade was
consummated and, having a chuckle or two with
Grandpa, we both relived the past, if for just a
very short while. I let the wife worry some
over my inexplicable smile for hours before I
poured out the story. Then we both shared the
mem'ry of the old green Berkley I bought shortly
after our wedding.

   Another time I was headed toward a glorious
week of hunting in the mountains when, on a
farmer's open field, I spotted an old Willys
Jeep. Rust had claimed title to a great
percentage of it but it sure looked like my
dad's old buster. The rust notwithstanding, I
saw a glistening paint job kept smiling through
constant care that pop lavished on the old
vehicle. It wasn't new when he got it; in fact
I think it was manufactured old. And I'd be
lying if I boasted it, "Never failed to get us
there." It did that aplenty but somehow dad
used to have it rolling in time to save the day.

   If cars could talk there'd be no stories of
bigger than usual fish or trophy bucks 'cause I
just figure a car wouldn't lie. But we sure had
a thousand good times in that old machine and
the farmer thought I was pure Looney Tunes when
I asked permission to slog through the mud just
to see the old car and drink in a number of
years worth of mem'ries.

   Then there was the time I packed my gear for
a fishing excursion to a now popular lake when I
thought maybe I ought to shave some of the
weight from the tackle box. I always bring a
ton of true debris in the box that wouldn't find
a use in the next millenium so I started to cull
out some of the stuff in there. Sure enough I
chucked things of limited usefulness into a
drawer when I spotted a lure, totally void of

tarnish or scratches. As I sat there I
recollected its history. My two sons had bought
me that lure when they were mere toddlers;
pooled their collection of pennies and exploded
with glee when I opened the small package
underneath a Christmas tree all asparkle with
lights and tinsel. I can hear the two of them
now, squealing, "Open it Daddy, it's real neat!"
I did and it *was* real neat.

I never used the lure for fear of its
becoming lost in the weeds as so many of my
lures do. Perhaps if their dad were a better
fisherman he'd take the chance. A gift given in
love couldn't possibly be a failure but I tell
you I'll never know. I only wish I knew which
would be my very last fishing trip because then
I'd try it. As for the kids, maybe they
remember that gift but I'll never forget it.
That's a mem'ry I'll take with me to the great
beyond.

Now I ask little of my readers; don't have a
right to. But I ask you now, when you come
across an object hurled out of the past, don't
dismiss it lightly. Bring back those mem'ries
and pause awhile. Life's too hurried anyway,
take a minute, you'll be glad you did.

My Daddy used to say, "Mem'ries 'r the only
things don't cost a nickel to collect."

CHAPTER 17

THE SHED

Funny thing about sheds; the minute you build the rascals they're filled with junk and you need another one. I built one in the backyard of my Bellnmore, New York home to alleviate a critical condition in the garage which had failed to house an automobile for some half dozen years and it magically filled up in twenty four hours. And...the garage is still full of Junk!

I had decided to build *the* shed which would solve my space problems and provide a home for some of my fishing gear and things like that. I carefully designed, put drawing to paper and itemized materials needed to build the ideal shed. I worked for a few days mashing nails erecting the formidable edifice. I've had a more or less passing acquaintance with the necessary tools to do the job. For instance, I already owned two pounders, a turner for screws, a driller and an electric motor blade thing for cutting boards. So you can see I was no novice.

Well, with the possible exception of a slight tilt angle, the structure resembled the shed of my dreams when completed and looked

quite good actually. I, on the other hand, had
bandages on three fingers, needed a back brace
for several weeks, and didn't look so good.

I wearily marched off to slumber expecting
to transfer my outdoor gear to the shed, sort of
garage junk turned into shed junk, in the
morning. When I awoke I found that my eldest
son, a perceptive youth, had discovered the shed
in the yard and had already stuffed it full with
his junk I wasn't even aware existed. So much
for getting the old Jeep in the garage!

My next attempt at shed construction was at
my little cabin in the woods of Vermont. The
need was plain as a car or truck had *never*
graced the tiny detached garage which was packed
to overflowing with mowing tractor, snow
thrower, fishing gear, hunting equipment, chain
saw, et al.

This project naturally came with a new level
of experience. I not only had built one
previously but was now fairly proficient with
pounders and turners. Drillers and electric
motor blade things still gave me a bit of
trouble but one forges on.

This shed will likely be standing long after
we've been blown to the great hunting camp in
the sky by an errant nuclear something or other.
I went to Wilcox Sawmill to get the fixin's and
found that at a sawmill a 2x4 is a 2x4! No
trimming or dressing is applied to the basic
slices from the tree. It also weighs
proportionately more than the skinny lumber yard
variety and they're cut from wood hard as rock.
The shed cost about $250 not counting the
deductible on a double hernia operation.

The shed worked out just fine but, in the
mysterium of sheds, filled up in roughly 24
hours, leaving me with the need for another
shed.

I waited several years, mostly spent
shuffling sporting gear around here and there,
before seriously considering the ultimate shed.

As a concession to age and a general lack of
ambition I inquired into pre-cut wooden sheds.
They turned out to be a bit of a problem. My
budget was somewhat deficient and my truck,
which had aged right along with me, would have
trouble with the some 1200 board feet of prime,
heavy-as-lead, timber offered. I almost hate to
confess it but I succumbed to a *metal* shed.
This was a cardinal error right from the start.

In any case I found the Sears and Roebuck,
on-sale-special, to be somewhat heavier than
advertised and the instructions rather amusing.

The first piece of advice directed that one
must put the building up in one day as it won't
stand by itself in an overnight breeze unless
completed! Right they are!

I trucked mine to the woods in the rain on a
brutal night and began construction the next
morning on a dreary but windless day. The base
for the shed took half a day and then I got to
the meat of the thing.

Almost simultaneously with the start of the
erection came the breeze. At least it started
as a breeze; progressing to wind and right
through to a gale. I don't know if you have
ever tried to put up one of these contraptions
by yourself, which is a study in patience for
starters, but in a wind it's a real test. The
material of which the thing is constructed is
about the gauge of hefty tissue paper.

The initial setting up of the flimsy siding
was, without a doubt, a miracle to behold. The
procedure is simple. First you need to hold the
gossamer siding in place with one hand and the
screw turner with the other. With your third
hand you insert the sheet metal screw and

tighten 'er right up. Multiply this procedure
by about three million screws and presto!, your
shed is complete.

During the process, naturally, it rained
once more and the temperature dropped to the
mid-thirties. Both conditions rare for the
season, and unpredicted by the radio weatherman
who, I've later been told, has that kind of
sense of humor and because of it, lives in a
home surrounded by guard dogs. Folks should pay
more attention to my outdoor plans and they
could dispense with the radio weatherman
altogether.

By the time I finally attached the last roof
panels and snapped a cheap padlock through the
rather impotent looking plastic door handles, my
hands resembled the hue of a freshly boiled
lobster.

After a dream-invaded sleep, I staggered out
to the metal wart on the landscape and popped
open the made-in-Taiwan lock. Somebody has got
to explain to me how it could have filled to the
brim overnight! Bicycles, lawnmowers, paint
cans, fishing rods, hunting boots; and my poor
old Jeep will spend the winter outside once more
as the garage is still choked wall to wall.
Maybe I just don't build 'em big enough?

My Daddy use to say, "I've got a champagne
and caviar appetite on a beer and pretzels
budget!"

CHAPTER 18

PLAIN BROWN WRAPPER

Every sportsman (or woman) comes across someone in his or her lifetime who becomes a sort of mentor. And it's been my experience that the truly great folks of this world are most often camouflaged. They come in a plain brown wrapper, as it were, and simply do wonderful things without 76 trombones and fanfare.

Such was a really special old timer I had the great good fortune to have known. He taught me more about outdoors and just plain livin' than anyone else. He was a mountain man and Norman Bentley, in my estimation, was a living legend.

When Norman was well past the four score mark in years he still put all my sportsman buddies and myself included, of course, to shame.

Any thoughts of a dancing career were erased at a young age for Norman by an axe in the knee. Anyone remember when logs were split by axes? Probably not. Now we bust up a woodlot with powerful gas driven chainsaws and split the chunks with hydraulic splitters. The pile is

then hauled away in pickup trucks with Dolby
stereos and Eddie Bauer designed seat covers.
Don't get me wrong though, there's nothing evil
in progress, but if you haven't experienced the
methods used while getting there, then you need
a Norman Bentley to light the path.

And when it came to big game hunting, back
then simply to put food on the table, not a
trophy on the wall of the den, things were
different too. Norman's dad gave him *one* bullet
with which to get his deer. Ammunition was
costly; there were no second chances. I use
three just to sight in each season. But by
golly, he came back with the venison every year
so far as I know.

His eyesight at better than eighty years was
nothing short of marvelous and he developed the
knack of spotting game and game signs that I
would foolishly stumble right by, never
noticing. On numerous trips up Shatterack
Mountain in his veteran Jeep, he'd stop and
point out "dustin' areas" where partridge rid
themselves of mites and turkey scratches where
they dug around for grubs. I remember returning
to his dooryard which opens onto a distant hill
after a trip for some firewood. Mr. Bentley
said, "How many ya' figure are up there?"

I thought to myself, "How many *what* are up
where?"

Then he continued, "How many turkey? Looks
to be about twelve or so." He knew I was not
with him on this.

He looked at me with a knowing expression,
turned and went into the house and brought out
binoculars for my younger eyes. Sure enough,
pointing them in the general direction of his
gaze I counted *exactly* a dozen turkeys; still
microscopic dots on the far hill.

Mr. Bentley is responsible for building some
four dozen buildings in his long and successful
career as well as a significant number of
bridges (my own humble cabin in the woods was
erected from logs right off the land by Mr. *and*
Mrs. Bentley who helped on many of the
projects).

Want the name of any bird, fish, or mammal
in the area? You'd ask Norman; he'd have the
information and a lot more. Want to know where
such-and-such road goes, why it goes there and
who uses it? You'd ask Norman. Got a simple
question like where the deer are and why? Again
you'd call Norman. How about why your spring
runs slow sometimes, why it rained when the
weatherman guaranteed picnic weather, why the
geese fly lower than usual, how a digital watch
works (oh, yes that too!), how come the bass
fishing slowed up at the lake or the best way to
start your seeds for a good crop; you'd ask
Norman.

Every minute with the Bentley's was an
education. I've sat on their porch and observed
fairly a thousand birds and he'd name the many
species. He'd point out the subtle differences
between two seemingly identical (to me anyway),
birds. What I'm trying to say is most of us
don't pay enough attention to things going on
around us. We want to get through life entirely
too fast only taking short breaks now and then
for a hurried vacation, then back to blasting
our way through the years again. Mr. Bentley
has taught me to look around some, take my time,
smell the roses, so to speak. And I've learned
to listen too. A chance to chat with folks like
the Bentley's is an opportunity that should
never be passed up. If you know someone like
Norman, I plead with you to take advantage of
the wisdom of years. If it leaves without being

passed on, it would be nothing short of a crime.
Something valuable and irretrievable stolen from
us for good.

A trip down memory lane with Norman was
always true instruction. Somehow with all our
progress from hand hewn furniture to space-age
plastics I think we've lost something. And Mr
Bentley showed me that though times were tougher
when he was my age, in some ways folks had more.
His love for family transcends our typical drive
for the dollar.

He's showed me what it is to be a survivor.
Life threw it's petty problems his way and he
deftly backhanded them over the net. He'd seen
cycle after cycle of what nature can dish out
and simply replayed the hand. And I hope when I
grow up (if ever), I could be just like him; a
bit stubborn, prone to tell a good tale maybe
more than once if someone will listen, and smart
enough to seek out youngsters to share my own
experiences. I also hope to be in tune with the
world around me and hunt and fish by the old
ethics.

And maybe you wonder about Mrs. Bentley?
Well here we have a most wonderful woman; and
expert at living life the best you can. Clara
is all any lady could ever hope to be. She's a
friendly, warm, giving person, always willing to
share, who's struggled with life and won; a
model for the rest of us who imagine the worst
thing in the world would be the VCR breaking
down.

If my wife, Julie, and I could together
accomplish one tenth of what the Bentleys have
I'd be tickled right pink. And yet they ask
nothing special. It's plain brown wrapper all
the way. Norman was taken from us recently
leaving a large void in many of our lives. And

I never minded the tales repeated; I just
enjoyed them more each time.

My Daddy used to say, "The flashiest grapes
don't always make the best wine."

CHAPTER 19

YEAH, CHARLIE, THEY WORK BUT...

Charlie Buckle is a guy who looks like what every kid would want for a grandfather. I don't know how old he is but he mentioned witnessing the Louisiana Purchase. He's easy to spot because he's always got an infectious smile which never seems to darken.

I've known Charlie for a few years and we swap outrageous fishing stories during the coffee intermission at Long Island Flyrodder's monthly meetings.

The fish caught gain inches and pounds at each telling as this is legal, nay, the duty of any self respecting fisherman and fly fishermen have more self respect than most. The flies these visionary fish were caught on go through their own sort of metamorphosis with the telling of the tale. The reason for selecting a particular fly will vary with wind direction, magnetic declination, presence or absence of moss on the North side of nearby trees, the Sol-Lunar tables and just plain intuition in addition to the mundane business of matching the hatch. Why any fisherman worth his salt, and

Charlie has been labeled "salty" at times, will
explain that after running about four hundred
variables through his mind's computer he decided
exactly what fly is required, I'll never know.
It's stretching things a might. And fumbling
through the disorganized box of flies extracted
from his vest pocket (amid a Snickers bar, a
soggy package of chewing gum, half a pair of
scissors and a crumpled tissue) lo and behold
there would be the perfect imitation; a hand
tied version of "the fly". The fly will, of
course have a name, although that's relatively
unimportant to the fish. I've yet to meet a fly
tyer of more than a few weeks proficiency who
didn't have a fly in his collection named after
some personal event, a favorite spot on the
river, or in the case of some narcissistic
folks, themselves. Well anyway this perfect fly
will be flung with varying degrees of expertise
and an unvarying degree of confidence. And so
the fish story has its modest beginnings.

So one night just before hunting season last
year Charlie says to me, "Hey, Al, you're with
those Fish and Game guys aren't you?"

"Sure, Charlie," I said, "but pipe down will
you, everybody will hear. I've still got some
credibility here, don't ruin it!"

Charlie knew that the Fish and Game
Association put on an annual demonstration of
proper field dressing of a whitetail deer. It's
open to the public and accomplished by experts
for the novice hunter. The deer is provided
under a special permit by the Department of
Environmental Conservation for educational
purposes and is generally a road kill. In any
case I asked my friend why this was of
particular interest. His reply was, "I'd like
you to get me a patch of the facial hair for
me."

Not knowing if he was a frustrated barber or
perhaps he had finally snapped a spring, I
queried as to why. He indicated that he had a
very special fly he wanted to tie. I pushed him
for details such as the name of the fly and how
it was tied but he wouldn't budge. He just sat
there with that once admired smile. So I said.
"No way!"

Then he stood and yelled, "Hey guys...listen
to this, Al here's a member of the..."

"Ok, ok, you win," I burst out in a
desperate attempt to save what's left of my
reputation. "You've got your hair."

The Big Game Night arrived and after the
entire deer was dressed and skillfully skinned I
opened my specially sharpened pocket knife and
nonchalantly snatched a goodly piece of the
facial hair from the left cheek. I did this
very carefully; no, not to avoid damaging the
material but to avoid detection by my hunting
buddies and instantly being labeled a pervert.
That's when, from just behind me, came a request
in a thunderous voice from a Charles McGuiness,
although I did not know the name at that
instant. He asked, "Yo, how about cutting me a
little patch from the other side there?"

I turned around to see *this* Charlie standing
six foot thirteen and a half inches tall and as
wide as a powder wagon. "Whatever you want,"
was my reply. I removed yet another swatch as
my curiosity was being piqued. I was real
curious now about this sudden interest in deer
cheeks. Maybe I missed a chapter in Eric
Leiser's new fly tying manual or something. So
I asked this large variety of McGuiness whether
he was indeed tying some very special fly (then
I could go back to that smart alec Buckle with a
name).

But he told me he hadn't even a suspicion of
what it was for, it was for his neighbor Charlie
Buckle.

Why that scoundrel! He put the word out all
over town. Didn't trust me eh? Figured at
least one of his emissaries would come back with
a chunk of cheek hair. Well now he would have
two patches and good riddance!

It turned out that both Charlie and I ended
up with a little unplanned time on our hands
after a bout with illnesses. So at the first
Flyrodder's meeting we attended, Charlie
generously handed me four of the slickest Caddis
imitations you've ever seen, fabricated from the
infamous deer facial hair. He told me it was
the speciality of Paul Shaeffer who is his good
friend and a Professor of fly tying at age 72,
just a few years younger than I felt at the
time. Paul apparently uses the concoctions in
the summer and fall exclusively, and primarily
late in the day. He did not give it a name that
I'm aware of so I call it the "Buckle." Fishing
with a "Buckle" could pose a small problem for a
fisherman if someone streamside asks, "Hey,
whatcha usin'?"

You say, "A Buckle." He thinks you're an
unsociable wiseguy. It's still better than
naming it the "Buzz Off".

Anyway I thanked Charlie and he made me
promise to report my success or failure with the
fly. I'm doing that right now essentially.
Firstly, let me tell you "Buckles" are trouble.
It started almost immediately. I brought the
little darlings home after the meeting and, the
hour being late, as they say, I put them in a
little bunch on the kitchen table to examine
more closely in the morning after I got both
eyes open at the same time. In the morning I
couldn't find them and I searched the table top

completely. My lovely spouse of some quarter century asked, "What on earth are you looking for, sit down and eat your gruel (her specialty).

"I had some very special flies tied by Charlie Buckle right here on the table. I know I put them there by the sugar bowl."

"Oh, those," she countered. "I swept up some bugs this morning." Have you ever searched through the garbage loaded with old lettuce leaves, a half eaten bologna sandwich, (gruel sneaked in while the cook's head was turned) and other assorted domestic trash? Well it ain't pretty. At least the flies looked real enough to sweep up. I was afraid they wouldn't any longer but three survived ok...I think one must have flown away.

I packed the little buggers in a separate fly box to take to Vermont to try out on my favorite section of the Battenkill. It was now spring and the trout season open. Off I went, arriving at dusk and in the dim light of the shed, tied one on a number five weight line with a 5x tippit to be ready first thing in the morning. But restless as I am I just had to throw a few practice casts in the pond in front of the cabin. Sure it was getting dark but just a few casts would make me sleep better. On the first back cast I got the surprise of my life. These flies were real foolers as I found I had a bat firmly stuck on the end of my 5x. Bats are not my favorite creatures in all the world at the best of times but connected to my fly line; no way. Back in the shed I tied on a new leader after setting the bat free, albeit with one of my "Buckles" and a length of leader. I was now down to two flies, I did not sleep well at all.

With great eagerness and anticipation I set out early in the morning, ignoring the many who

claim this is not the best time for fishing for
trout. With my rod nestled snugly next to me in
the truck, at the ready, with a 5x tippet back
in place adorned with my next to last deer cheek
hair fly, I headed for the section of the
Batenkill which I knew fairly well after having
fished it on and off for about twenty years. I
was also ignoring both the summer and fall
disclaimers and the "especially late in the day"
proviso passed on by Charlie. But who ever
really knows what a trout will want at any given
time right?

Now there are two approaches one can take
here. You either enter at the Salem Fish and
Game Club, assuming you are a member, which I
have been for many years, and fish upstream like
a normal person or you can go up stream to the
nearest access point, about a half mile up
river, and wade down, wait a bit for things to
quiet down, and then fish back up. Which would
you choose? The trade off here is that it had
rained for a whole day before and the embankment
to the stream by the Fish and Game Club is steep
and tricky at best.

I took the normal person route and managed
to get down, let's say, rather quicker than
expected, and was congratulating myself on my
great good fortune of survival in one unbroken
piece when I noticed that my fly had become
disconnected from the hook holder and was now
firmly attached to a bush at the top of the
embankment. Climbing back up that slimy, oil-
like cliff would be impossible. With great
regret, a tribute to being clumsy, I tied on my
last fly to my one remaining tippet which,
unfortunately was a very slim 7x.

At about a hundred yards I spotted a new
blowdown on the left bank which could have been
a picture from any beginner's book on fly

fishing. It was perfect right down to the eddy currents and jungle of limbs creating a pool that *had* to hold a trout; maybe even a big one. The debate went on in my head whether to risk my last fly on this almost certain spot or move on to less dangerous water. Even as the argument raged I had begun my back cast (I rarely listen to myself anyway). To my amazement I watched as the little fur blob headed exactly in between the greedy twigs all eager to rob me of my final "Buckle".

To this day, as I replay the scene in my mind, I'm convinced that fly never even touched down before a large brown trout smashed it. Maybe no record fish but certainly one of the biggest to ever get stuck on my tackle. Playing him was wonderful until he deftly created slack and sounded for the underwater world of tangles separating my 7x. Staring at the limp remnant with a tear in my eye I thought, "Yeah, Charlie, they do work but...I have none left!" Forgive the play on words but there's no telling how many fish I could have landed if I had even just one more Buckle on my vest.

My Daddy used to say, "There's no point in being a fool if you can't prove it now and again."

CHAPTER 20

TRAILERIN'

One thing every outdoorsman
(outdoorsperson?) gets familiar with quickly is
trailers. Some wield huge forty foot outsized
monsters to take the whole family cross country,
others tug a tiny pop-up type behind the pickup
and have all they need to survive hunting,
camping, and fishing trips about anywhere in the
Milky Way. My experience with trailers began
(and nearly ended) with a teensy weensy soft
covered tug-along towed behind a station wagon.
    I bought the thing second hand for about two
hundred bucks and had it for a number of
reasonably enjoyable years before a wind storm
up in Maine on a hunting trip reduced it to
scrap. I practiced at night when I first got it
so the neighbors wouldn't laugh themselves ill
watching me back it into the driveway. Some of
those same folks would likely pile in it on
fishing excursions in a short while and I
figured to be adept at hauling the thing by then
    At first it took a mere eleven tries to back
the contraption up the drive and a few scary
moments trying to judge the distance left
between the garage door and the back of my pop-

up. Ask anyone who tows a trailer and they'll
tell you instinct is just exactly backwards when
you first start trailerin'. Am I right? You
automatically pull the wheel one way, the
trailer goes the other and you're ready for
another try. But after a while I was ready to
put the thing on the open road come what may.

In all my adventurous travels I have never
had a problem getting out of my home town. I've
driven now for almost thirty five years and
every time...straight out, no problem. Oh,
sure, there have been problems along the way
with bridges, tunnels, overturned trucks,
spills, accidents, and other tie-ups but not
right in town. Well the first trip out with my
little trailer I headed towards the Expressway
and on a side street, half way down the block, I
found a guy dressed in patches of blaze orange
waving me to a halt. It seemed they had the
street opened like a raw wound looking for a gas
pipe or something. He said, "You'll have ta'
turn around there fella." These, the most
dreaded words possible to a new trailer captain.
I could see they picked a real dim bulb for a
flag holder here, 'cause he clearly didn't
understand the magnitude of his request!

And believe me, I tried. I went back and
forth, using about six gallons of gas and
finally figured I might just wait 'til they
fixed the stupid pipe. After all I was equipped
to camp right there for a week or more. The
very worst scenario would have been for my
neighborhood chums to spot my trailer laying
like a beached whale about a half mile from
ground zero. After swallowing a large lump of
pride and ignoring the snickering of the mental
giant with the flag, I unhitched my colossus
from the back of my wagon, pushed it aside,
turned both the wagon and the trailer around and

headed off into the sunset toward my goal,
totally oblivious to the belly bending laughter
going on around the hole in the street.

Since that time I've gotten somewhat better
and had many happy trips in my pop-up but, like
I say, it disintegrated in a storm and all
thoughts of trailerin' were subdued for some
time, until I simply needed one to transport
some heavy gear up to my cabin nestled in the
trees of Vermont.

In order to do this, I borrowed the "trailer
that Jeff built." Jeff being Jeff Fox; good
friend, sportsman, inventor, teller of
incredible tales and one-time trailer builder.
The trailer was fabricated on the premise that
one should never suffer the indignity of running
out of trailer space. To this end it was
plastered together in roughly the same detail as
a cattle car and had available about a quarter
acre confined by removable stake body sides...if
you happen to be able to remove about four
hundred pounds of stake body!

Anyway, I left with the sun setting in
March, skies clear, temperature hovering around
freezing and roads dry. I left the homestead
and waved, smiling and gleeful to my wife and
kids, as they could not make the trip, I was
thankful there was nary a trace of snow about as
there had been a week prior.

I buzzed along listening to the radio and
popping coins in toll machines until, somewhere
in upstate New York, I was jolted awake by the
fact that I had been driving with no notice of
the six or eight inches of snow alongside the
road. And things got worse.

Rolling along Route 22 with my eyes abulge
by now with a wind raging and the road icy, the
inevitable happened; someone a few cars ahead
stopped to avoid a collision with a clown

entering from a side road. My trailer and I
tried to do the same, but my tires said, "Not
today, old buddy." We sailed ahead. Next scene
showed me steering off the road into the snow to
miss the car in front and skidded by, I swear,
faster than when I hit the hooks! I couldn't
resist a big smile as I zipped past each driver
and when I hit solid ground, I jumped on the
throttle and, in effect, passed them all like a
Keystone Cop film. It actually took less than a
half hour for my heart beat to come down to just
below life threatening.

    Then further on, now snowing gayly, traffic
stopped as emergency vehicles gathered to
retrieve a monstrous wing plow that descended
over the side of the road. For style points I
gave him a 9.5 and a degree of difficulty of 2.
Execution was sloppy though; 6.0. So here I was
stuck again, when this fellow steps up and says,
"Sorry, guess you'll have to turn around." This
seemed like Deja Vu. I eyeballed the narrowness
of Route 22 and decided I would likely be right
down there with the wing plow. I was fully
prepared to wait 'til spring when, with the
beginnings of a tear in my eye, I finally asked
if there wasn't any other way around the
calamity. This guy, who had to be a real weak
signal, says, "Oh, yeah. That road there
(pointing to a road winding up a hill rivaling
the Matterhorn), but it's sort of private; folks
don't like traffic on it. Takes ya' right
beyond the accident back onto Route 22." The
road he alluded to was a vertical impossibility
covered in snow...but it's mouth was only ten
yards from the front of my eager four wheel
drive truck. Immediately as he pointed out the
alternate route I made my plan. By now I'm sure
he's figured out that he may have been hasty in
sharing such a confidence.

I said, "Oh, well, that's the breaks," and
sauntered to the cab of the old truck,
nonchalantly started the motor, checked the
shift for four wheel engagement and rolled down
the window a few inches. I then shouted,
"Geronimo...Look out!", popped the clutch and
threw rooster tails of snow left and right on my
way up the forbidden hill. I swayed, slipped,
plunged, and surged to the crest and then zoomed
down the other side; the trailer creating a fury
all it's own. Then halfway down, I recognized
another potential problem. Apparently my plan,
as it unfolded in front of God and everybody,
was spotted by other frustrated motorists and I
now had company; slipping and sliding in my
tracks, just inches from the trailer.

Back on Route 22 things calmed down and I
began to feel invincible. You know how it is
after a harrowing scare; all of a sudden you
begin to think you handled that pretty well.
For the rest of the trip I did real fine...until
I confronted the dirt road leading to my cabin
in the woods. Now we're talkin' serious snow
here! God bless the town folks who plow this
road regularly and had piled a mound of snow
across my drive entryway which had melted and
refrozen into a hill roughly three feet high;
only I didn't know about the frozen part. I got
up a head of steam, as it were, poured on the
coals and headed for the driveway. Had I been
stopped by the mini-mountain there would have
been no problem but I made it half way over. At
that exact moment I realized what the four wheel
magazines refer to as "high centering". I was
"high centered" alright. I was "high centered"
for hours, in fact. All this time as I dug,
chopped, and jacked up various places, the
trailer was sticking well out onto the road. I
considered setting it on fire but I didn't. I

was close to terminally exhausted when Chuck, the mailman, churned up the road and tugged me off the mound with his four-by-four vehicle. I finally busted through the ice, got the trailer unloaded and stumbled into the cabin, cold and almost delirious.

I don't believe I'll ever tow a trailer again if you don't mind!

My Daddy used to say, "When you're towing a trailer, don't worry, all your troubles are behind you."

CHAPTER 21

DEAR SANTA:

Dear Santa:

Much as I truly hate to complain I find I must mention that last Christmas was certainly a disappointment. Now I'm surely not one to hold a grudge and I won't mention it further but it would do wonders if you could pay some special attention to my list this year. As for that unfortunate lapse last year I am aware you had just computerized your operation and that you are forced to work with elves (believe me there are a few in my office too so I know!). And when I called I realized that Mrs. Claus seemed to have a doozey of a cold so I understand (by the way, that *was* Mrs. Claus that answered the phone right? Just kidding, ho, ho, ho.).

Anyway, this year I feel more or less entitled to some special consideration and a Sturm Ruger Red Label Over and Under would be very well received and appreciated. To make matters easier I should mention that my wife has Visa and Mastercharge (as well as Macy's, Alexander's, Discover, American Express and Diner's Club so there should be no problem), and

has shown little or no reluctance to using same.
Perhaps I didn't point this out in my letter
last year which may have contributed to the mix-
up but, hey, I said I wouldn't mention it again
and I won't. By the way the Red Label Over and
Under will be listed under "N" for necessity and
not the usual luxury category as I'll explain.

My trap and skeet scores have fallen off
dramatically in the last two years. I had plans
to correct this situation last year with the new
gun but then I've covered the reason why that
didn't happen earlier so I won't repeat myself
here like I promised, ok? As with any shooter I
was convinced the problem was with my gun which
is old and in need of replacement, for about two
years now in my estimation if you get my drift,
and certainly not with my technique.

However, being a fair minded sportsman I
thought a scientific test and a little research
would settle the issue. As I indicated, I'm
just about a year off my schedule but, not to
worry, I'm a patient man. So like I said, I
researched the Red Label and it states very
clearly in the full color ad that the gun is an
engineering masterpiece and performs
beautifully. These folks wouldn't fib would
they? At least not this close to Christmas
where Santa would be likely to find out and
probably not forget for a very long time. In
fact your memory is legendary which is why it is
such a puzzle how you could have forgotten my
address last year but I guess these things
happen. The important thing is that we not
repeat our errors right? Well, with the
research completed I visited an establishment
which specializes in equipment of the type
referred to here and, for several glorious
moments, sighted along the gleaming barrel of
the Red Label Over and Under and it was this

empirical evidence that finally convinced me
that this would be the answer to my falling
scores. And, further, call it fate if you like,
the gun exactly fits my reach right out of the
box! You'd think this gun was made for me
alone. Well, maybe *you* wouldn't think this but
that's just an expression we use, you know? I
surely didn't mean to insult your intuition
there.

And, though I for certain, wouldn't resort
to a such a tactic, I could mention the time
when I was seven and wanted that Daisy Red Rider
BB gun. Remember? I waited three full years.
Three full years of being good, I might add, for
that gun, but, again, I normally wouldn't have
even brought it up except perhaps it's time to
get things straightened out. I mean I was
almost ready for an electric shaver by the time
I got that BB gun. If the Red Label Over and
Under isn't more timely I'm afraid my scores
will be so abysmal that there will be no hope.
Depression may very well set in disrupting my
entire family life and that would not really be
fair to them, don't you think? I wouldn't want
anyone of your stature to harbor guilt of that
magnitude on my account.

To simplify things I'm leaving a copy of
this letter on my wife's sewing machine. She
is, as you probably know 'cause you're supposed
to know stuff like this, without a doubt a
darling mate and is sharp enough to realize the
importance of this one item on my list. As a
matter of fact she is the best wife a guy could
have and will likely be contacting you very
shortly about the matter of the Red Label gun,
as I will be about the new coat she has
requested for Christmas.

Finally there's this matter of naughty or
nice. While I'm sure you know, I'll save you

the trouble of looking it up and tell you right
off I've been good all year. Well...maybe not
all year but recently I've been super. I left
hunting camp to be home with the family for
Thanksgiving dinner, picked up all my clothes
from the floor and have eaten all my vegetables.
Honest.

Oh, and by the way, please don't use the
chimney this year. Last year, as I say, I was
prepared and had the thing squeaky clean but,
alas, to no avail as you chose to skip my visit
and I hate to bring it up again but I do it
merely to inform you that this year with all my
doing good and all I've simply had no time to
get to it. I wouldn't like to be responsible
for soot on your fine red suit (or the cleaning
bill, ho, ho ho). By the way, where ever did
you get that suit? I mean it's you! But I
don't intend to flatter, all I proposed to do
was suggest that maybe UPS would, in the long
run, be best, reindeer notwithstanding and don't
get me wrong, they're terribly cute. I would
never, ever shoot at one even during the open
season though it would surely be a clean shot
with a Red Label if you take my meaning, but
then I digress don't I?

And while on the matter of delivery, I was
going to enclose a check to cover the shipping
and handling up front but I sealed the envelope
before I thought of it.

> Looking forward to your
> visit, (not like last year
> but then, I really don't
> want to mention it again).

> Al Westbrook

CHAPTER 22

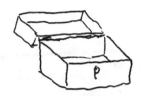

IT'S AROUND HERE SOME PLACE

Being organized is a gift. However, my life has always been governed by what I call the 80-20 rule. This rule, based on heavy duty scientific research, claims that we do 80 per cent of what we do using 20% of our available resources. Put another way it means if I've used a tool, reference book or map, for instance, I'm very likely to use it again. So why put it away? But organization is deeper rooted and "some folks got it and some folks ain't", as they say. I ain't!

My neighbor Ralph Gillies, makes me physically ill whenever we go fishing and he opens his tackle box. Each row of little compartments in the many tiered trays holds but one type of lure arranged by color, size, and intended prey. A quick glance across the box looks like the color sample charts you paw over when choosing paint for the living room walls. The left most will be a dark green, the next will be a lighter shade, then fading to yellow and on to the reds at the other end of the box.

And down below he has his several line weights actually spooled and ready. And in a

special section, all by itself, is a book of
hand-tied flies with all the falderal necessary
to match the hatch if the occasion should arise.
It's a shame some people have to live like this.
I figure it's like a sickness that they simply
can't shake.

In slight contrast to Ralph's is my own
tackle box. My lures are assembled in my
patented "lure lump". That is, all my lures are
fastened together by a magical intertwining of
hooks and barbs. In order to select the lure of
choice I simply pick up the mass by one of the
pigtails of monofilament left on many for the
purpose (which covers for being too lazy to snip
it free) and spin the glob of lures until the
chosen one passes by. I then merely pluck it
from the group. And since the plucking method
has failed a significant number of times I've
got a fallback plan. In such a case you just
drop the "lure lump" in the gravel and kick it
about until the proper lure swings free.

The little trays on top will invariably
contain a museum-like collection of dried worms
stuck indelibly to the tray and each other. I
did not *buy* them dried; they were once live,
thrashing worms. The history of my fishing
trips where worms were used can be traced here
as surely as the probe for the evolution of man
but on a far less grand scale. That, in a
nutshell, is why I've never chiseled them out.

Down in the bottom, nestled between last
trip's bologna sandwich and the spoiled puddle
of salmon eggs, is my spare mono line. It is
not spooled, although it may have been so at one
time. It is unlikely that it will ever be so
again but the attempt should provide several
hours of amusement if not lively conversation.

Some hunters, too, amaze me with their
organizational acumen. A study of their

backpacks is an awe inspiring experience. I've
seen guys with their compass, whistle and first
aid kit tucked neatly in one pocket, ammunition,
pen, handwarmers, or binoculars tucked deftly in
another. Then down inside is the hot seat, a
portable, three burner stove, napkins, paper
plates, side of beef, coffee, tea, freeze dried
milk, shaving kit and drag rope (I've never
needed one of these yet). The whole thing
measures just eight inches by 12 inches and
nestles comfortably, being well balanced, in the
center of the back.

My own typical hunting day will find me well
up the mountain when I discover compass,
whistle, et al., is on the top of the bureau
back at the cabin. Roughly noon time will be
when the thermos of steaming hot coffee will
make its absence noted as it sits on the kitchen
table alongside my ammunition which will not be
recognized until a six point buck errs his way
into my sights. The resounding click, repeated
several times has been thought to almost scare a
buck to death. In fact one year, hunting
unknowingly in the vicinity of a famous doctor,
caused him to take note of the sound and create
a duplicate in the lab which is now used to
pulverize kidney stones. But do I get any
credit? No!

There are boaters I know who are affected by
organization also. Having had my own boat for
years I can recognize it right off. This fellow
I work with invites me out on his boat quite
often and I must say his boat differs from what
mine was.

Firstly, they have to hang a sign up at his
slip, "Caution, do not look directly at this
boat in bright sunlight!" It's polished and
waxed like a new car and fairly gleams in the
water. My own rig was covered with so much

marine life it was almost camouflaged. I always
meant to get to it you know but something always
came up, like making sure the fishing poles were
in a decent pile below.

When I first stepped onto the boat I said,
"Harry, your boat's empty! You've got nothing
on it. I better run back home and get some
poles, bait, a cooler of vittles, stuff like
that." That's when he proudly took me below
deck. He actually had all that stowed away! I
was familiar with it being up on deck, here and
there; handy sort of. His anchor ropes were
coiled neatly out of the way on a shiny bow.
Mine were basically in a ball but only the part
not actually tied to something so what's the
diff? And my bow was far from shiny having been
decorated by both former minnows and gifts from
the sea gulls, but slippery it was not. Why if
your sneakers got uppity you wouldn't slide four
inches before your foot would hook a chunk of
dried bait stuck to the surface and presto, your
slide would be arrested. Safety first.

An outdoor sport with unique organizational
challenge is skiing. Since I could never afford
more than a few one-day excursions separated by
several paychecks, things have a way of getting
a bit our of order. But there are benefits.

For example, a buddy calls you at 9 P.M.,
"Hey Al, what say we play hookey tomorrow and
get in a day of skiing? It's supposed to snow
some more and we'll get weekday ticket prices.
What say?"

Of course you can't pass this up. So you
have to sell some of the furniture to pay for
it, what the heck. Besides the guy loves to
drive his new Lincoln.

So now I head for the closet and locate one
ski and an unmatched pair of gloves with holes
in at least three fingers; both lefts. It's at

this point that I begin the beneficial aerobic
exercise of turning every closet in the house
inside out in search of the rest of the gear.
This usually lasts a minimum of two hours giving
me enough time to lash it all together and get a
few hours sleep before my companion shows up in
the pre-heated Lincoln at 5:30 in the A and M.
I will have had at least a good cardiac workout
whereas the neatnic who can just reach into the
hall closet and grab all his gear in one swoop
is tinkering with his health.

Well I guess I'm just stuck with the way I
am. I'll always have my nails and screws in one
coffee can, if indeed they ever make it to the
coffee can, and my charge card receipts for 1986
will be mixed up with 1966. When I go fishing I
may leave my lunch home on the kitchen table but
then I'll have the apple and chocolate bar I
forgot to take out of the box from last trip; it
works out. And I'll never tire of the surprise
of finding vacant spaces in my socket wrench
box. Such is life.

My Daddy used to say, "Don't worry, it'll be
in the very last place you look."

CHAPTER 23

WALKIN' IN MY RUNNING SHOES

Yessir, I'm aware we live in the age of rockets, epoxy, VCR's, and space age plastics but that doesn't mean everything's roses. Those rockets' value is dubious to the average sportsman (he or she that is), epoxy always gets in the wrong places and does not lift a Jeep like it says on TV, and burning plastics in our trash has been an unfortunate demon for our atmosphere. I think I was just plain born too late; I simply don't fit, like an oval peg in a round hole. Progress has complicated my life forcing painful decisions.

Why in the area of sports clothing alone there's still a revolution going on. When I was a lad my Dad had one hunting coat and one wooly hunting shirt, thick as a horse blanket. They were both red and black plaid and did the job just fine according to Pop. Ok, so they weighed slightly less than a lead alloy but, golly, they lasted year after year showing little signs of wear from rough use in the woods. He wore a wool cap and L.L. Bean boots on every big game hunting trip I can recall. In summer there was a green roll-up felt hat with a few fishing

flies stuck into the band. In the history books
my kids' kids will get in school, this will be
remembered as The Pre-Gortex Era.

Now, however, a sportsman is forced to make
choices. They're not always easy either. You
can select, for instance, the traditional red-
black plaid, green-black plaid, plain red,
camouflaged, in either the standard or the tree
bark models, blaze orange or reversible khaki;
hunting coats can be had in either wool, nylon,
Dacron, anythingcron or Gortex. See what I
mean?

Everything is billed as 'light as a
feather', 'waterproof' and 'breathable' these
days. I love that 'breathable'; are they
telling me dad's jacket suffocated? He never
once mentioned even hearing it cough much less
gag.

You can now get hunting and/or fishing hats
with wide brims, long bills, peaked, blaze
orange, cammo, or any color of the rainbow with
either mesh back or solid on the ball cap
styles. And on the front of these they'll print
just about anything within very wide limits of
decency.

I'm tempted to laugh out loud every time I
go downhill skiing and see in front of me on the
lift lines, a million dollar collection of ski
clothing in the most outrageous colors and
stuffed with down, Hollofil, Polar Silk,
Polartec fleece; lined with nylon, rayon or the
ever popular Gortex again. While I'm holding
back my giggles I hear some sniggering in my
direction as I stand in my denim jeans and red-
black checkered hunting coat. So I'm wet and
cold, that's what winter sports are all about
right?

And now there's a specialized selection of
gloves you wouldn't believe. There's hunting

gloves, mittens, shooting mittens with a flap
for the trigger finger to pop out like a Jack-
in-the-box, baseball gloves, driving gloves,
golfing gloves, and ordinary cowhide gloves like
my dad had. Sure your hands froze in the winter
and sweated some in the summer but they wore
like iron and gained what dad called 'character'
right up to the day your index finger finally
popped through the worn spot near the seam.

Then there's shooting vests and fishing
vests in various styles and varieties adapted to
the two sports. They come in four, six or eight
pockets, zippered, buttoned and Velcroed;
fabric, leather or mesh; shooters can get
shoulder patches for either left or right handed
use. The catalogues boggle your mind;
decisions, decisions.

And you can get waders with stocking foot,
boot foot, felt bottom, chain tread, or corkers.
They can be rubberized cloth, neoprene, 330
denier nylon (as in, "Don't be late for denier!"
Sorry.), Spandura, Cordura, or the kind I have,
made of truck tire rubber heavy as grandma's
dumplings and have to be patched after each
trip. Gives a fisherman something to do at
night.

Oh, and boots. Ever look at the boot
offerings in catalogues like *Cabela's*, *Gander
Mountain, Inc.*, *L.L. Bean* or *The Sportsman's
Guide*?

There's hiking boots, hunting boots, work
boots, climbing boots, rubber boots, leather
boots, Gortex boots, ski boots and even *after*
skiing boots. Boots can be had in six, eight or
ten inch heights, lined or unlined, insulated or
not, with lacing holes, rings or speed lacing
hooks. A guy needs half a dozen pairs of
different boots to be fashionable in the field
these days.

Shoes are a real culprit. How many pairs of shoes did you have when you were a kid? I don't know about girls (I was admonished to *never* peek into my sister's closet under the most severe kind of penalty; my sister's admonishment, of course), but I had two pairs. There was a pair of tight, wickedly painful and stiff monsters I was forced to wear to church and a wonderfully comfortable but tattered pair of U.S. Keds which I wore everywhere else. You remember, they had the little black circles at the ankles and they let you leap about ten feet or run from old Mrs. McGonagle's grasp when she caught you taking the short cut to the pond via her dooryard. You could do anything in a pair of U.S. Keds; beat the surf, race a train, break away from Ralphie Gilles's headlocks at school; anything.

But today there's walking shoes, running shoes, tennis shoes, deck shoes, golf shoes, wading shoes and baseball shoes. I wouldn't be surprised to see archery shoes, skeet shoes, or muzzleloading shoes turn up in the next set of catalogues.

Like I said, though, progress is like fingers; I didn't like it at first but they grow on ya'. So I'll pine some for the good old days but I still feel guilty when I look down and discover I'm walkin' in my running shoes.

My Daddy used to say, "As long as you're not going to get it, you might as well not get the very best."

CHAPTER 24

GLADYS AND THE COWBOY

True love is basically only found on Channel four and seldom interferes with real life. But examples are occasionally discovered in very unlikely places and very unlikely people. Such was the case with Gladys and the Cowboy.

With spring not far off I am reminded of a long, lanky friend of mine who used to join us on an occasional fishing jaunt. We called him Cowboy for reasons long since forgotten. He did have a "cowboy" look about him, though, and gave off a perfume, the aroma of which is possibly connected with cows. Now I, myself, would never win any beauty contests but Cowboy wouldn't even be allowed to enter. He had a nose that could double as a weather vane and just a tufted fringe of hair outlining a massive bald spot on top of his head. He looked vaguely like a Monk wearing a comic's plastic schnozola.

Cowboy was a loner, preferring to pursue outdoor sports that did not require a crowd. His favorite avocation was rabbit hunting. He would eagerly await the opening of the seasons for both varying hare and cottontails with the same anxiety as a child waits for Christmas.

Now Gladys owned a diner, having had it forced on...er...bequeathed to her by her parents who, in the final moments showed their lack of humor by leaving the diner to Gladys. Neither Gladys nor the diner were particularly fun to look at. Gladys had ears whose shadow could keep a team of wild oxen cool in the summer, and long stringy hair. I suppose her figure to be O.K., but it's hard to tell as she always wore clothes that would be considered fashionable in downtown Kirensk. I'll just cut the description short here lest I run out of good things to say and have to get to her less attractive features.

The diner was not much to look at either and inappropriately named *Betty,s Truck Stop*. The name was inappropriate for a couple of reasons; a "Betty" hadn't set foot in *Betty's Truck Stop* since some time before the Revolution (it now being patroned only by grungy old hunters and fishermen et al.) and further a real truck hadn't stopped there *ever* if local scuttlebut can be trusted. A truck driver simply can't function with endless belching fits and heartburn that could light up Cincinnati.

Betty's Truck Stop, however, just happens to be on the way to a favorite fishing spot a few of our bunch use quite often. Some might accuse us of simply practicing our fly casting judging by the scarcity of fish produced, but it's a nice area. The monotony of things cooked over an open campfire necessitates a stop at *Betty's* and the risk of ptomaine adds to the adventure. Besides, *Betty's* is the only eatery in those parts. And... everybody likes Gladys.

Gladys, as if to make up for her singular lack of cooking skills, is an excellent rabbit huntress. Hasenpfeffer is sometimes even on the

menu in times of plenty but tastes like her
chicken which tastes like cardboard.

Gladys and the Cowboy had never met as he
never, blessed with great good fortune be he,
set foot inside the infamous truck stop and she,
except for forages for hare, rarely set foot
outside the place.

One day Cowboy was up and about assailing
the rabbit population in a new six inch snow
fall. As he panned the landscape he was brought
up short by a solitary figure standing some
distance off sporting a long gun and *longer
hair*. Then a rabbit broke out and ran its zig-
zag way across the field. Two shots rang out;
bang! boom! loud and clear and the two figures
moved toward the now former rabbit, as it were.
That's when Gladys and the Cowboy formally met.
Two shots; one rabbit. These were ingredients
for an argument that melted snow for a hundred
yards around.

The brooha subsided and the discussion more
calmly pursued back at *Betty's Truck Stop* where,
over gruel-like bowls of rabbit stew, product of
a recent successful hunt, other things were
introduced into the conversation.

Cowboy didn't drop in at *Clancy's Tavern*
much after that, at first feigning apathy but
later discovered making rather frequent long
trips upstate which just happened to deposit his
lanky frame on a stool at *Betty's Truck Stop*.

Then several miracles happened. One would
have been quite sufficient but an overabundance
of miracles occurred. First, Cowboy bought a
wig, spruced up his appearance and even bought a
new plaid shirt. He looked almost human.

Secondly, a trip to *Betty's* disclosed
someone new behind the counter. "Where's Glad?",
we all asked as we entered and began to wipe
food stains off the stools as usual, only to

find them sparkling which was amazing in its own
small way but the young girl that turned around
to answer the question, all laden with lipstick,
eyeliner and newly permed hair *was* Gladys! Hoo
boy, what a surprise! But the really good news
was the apparent attention to the menu. A bowl
of chili was now a tasty admix of flavors and
spicy ingredients in place of the murky,
smoldering, coagulating mass of mysterious items
often suspected of being grown in another world.
The spaghetti which used to somehow refuse to
divide itself into individual strands was now a
springy collection of savoruous strings
fragrantly vaporous like a picture in a magazine
ad. How on earth had all this happened? One in
our fishing group, with intellect above our
average (an IQ figure somewhere in the
neighborhood of a good football score), an
import from the Big Apple, said true love could
do such strange and wondrous things. "Nah", we
said in unison, none of us having been attacked
buy a bout of true love in three decades.

In any case Gladys and the Cowboy announced
their wedding plans shortly thereafter. We
tried to talk to the lad but he just wouldn't
listen. Beg, plead, nothing worked. Free chili
has that effect on some guys. *Clancy's* lost a
good, if somber, patron but *Betty's Truck Stop*
actually became a dispenser of acceptable food
and now even had a waiter. True love conquers
all, or at least chili and spaghetti.

My Daddy used to say, "A loaf of bread, a
jug of wine and thou be darned! Make it two
jugs and you got a deal."

CHAPTER 25

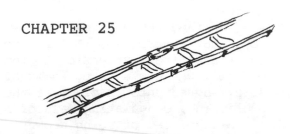

ON THE RIGHT TRACK

One of my favorite fishing spots is along
Mill Brook in Vermont. It also has a pretty
fair grouse population not far from its edges.
In order to get downstream to a reasonably sane
entry point one has to walk about a half mile
from the nearest vehicle parking area along a
railroad bed that once was pounded by massive
freight trains on the steel rails of the
Delaware & Hudson line. Many years ago the
rails were removed leaving some thirteen miles
of cinder roadbed from the New York border to
Pawlet Vermont. Mill Brook runs through a
little town called West Rupert that boasts a
population of 267 people and 1289 cows.

On my first excursion, while still virtually
a novice at fly fishing, I walked the distance
in my rubber soled waders and entered the brook
at a convenient spot opposite a large farm
field. That's where I found out that rubber
soled waders are almost worthless in these rock
strewn waters. The rocks were slicker'n a wet
bar of soap. Every step was an adventure and I
struggled my way about a half mile upstream,
roughly even with the spot where I'd parked my

truck adjacent to the lamp factory. The lamp
factory used to be a saw mill which originally
received its power from the mighty Mill Brook,
probably a hundred and fifty years or so ago. I
thought I'd just step out and cover what had to
be a short distance to the truck. Good plan
except for the fence. In the greenery
surrounding the brook the farmer, one Luke
Atwood, apparently put up this barbed wire fence
to keep his cows from crossing the stream and
meandering off God knows where.

     The only solution I could come up with was
to fish back downstream and get out somewhere
near where I'd gained access in the first place.
I had the same dismal luck as far as catching
fish on the way back as I did coming upstream.
When I got to that spot, however, facing
downstream this time, I could see the ideal pool
just around a short bend. This is the one you
see drawn in the *How To Read The Water* books.
It was perfect; strewn with good sized rocks at
the head end and a gorgeous riffle at the tail.
So, naturally I had to give it a try.

     I like to fish upstream with dry flies
although I know folks who do well in the
opposite direction; ergo, I climbed back out and
walked the railroad bed a little bit so I could
fish upstream to the pool. It took a while to
find a hole in the barbed wire fence which
reappeared but I prevailed and slid down the
embankment to the water's edge. I rather
hurried the fishing now, anxious to come within
sight of the pool.

     Up above on the farmers side of the
embankment there came in view a bunch of those
residents which West Rupert is famous for; cows.
My, they made an awful racket but I paid them
little attention. I was headed for *the* pool.

Finally I rounded a bend and there was that beautiful, idyllic fishing spot right in front of me. And standing hip deep in *my* pool was Betsy! A lone cow was stomping around in the most wonderful pool I'd seen in a long time. Foiled! She looked about to be joined by a gaggle of her sisters so I headed downsrtream once more.

Now I had to find a break in the fence again. Downstream I had a more difficult time with the wading as the rocks were round like bowling balls, planted there by some Divine perversion. The pressure of the water on the back of my legs added to the uncertainty of each miniscule step. Lifting a leg, it would shoot out and want to sail off into the sunset. It took a determined effort to get it back down where it belonged.

Just as I spotted a rent in the fence I noticed some activity up on the rise. Another fisherman, a very unusual thing to see on this little brook, was also walking the roadbed. He waved, and at the same time two lady joggers were coming down the trail. They waved. I'm friendly; I waved. In doing so on top of one of those bowling balls, I executed a nifty full gainer with a one and a half twist; degree of difficulty 7.5. I lost points on technical merit I'm sure but probably did well on style. Timing is everything they say and I had an audience of three; possibly the most people ever to assemble on that trail in any one spot *ever*. Go figure.

I tried to look nonchalant resting on my keester in three feet of water just a fraction of a degree above freezing; my waders filling with the icy liquid. I bade them, "Have a nice day." Their giggling put the fish down for hours.

The fisherman, when I finally did gain the
top of the slope, soaking wet and embarrassed,
was friendly and helpful. He explained about
felt sole waders which has opened up a whole new
horizon to my fishing. Don't leave home without
'em.
   Walking back to the truck fatigue set in
rapidly and each step felt like a ton. Each leg
seemed heavy as lead when in actuality they
weighed only as much as water. Draining my
waders helped immensely. During the trek I
mused silently about ancient history; how those
slippery rocks have probably been there for eons
being scrubbed smooth as glass by a continuous
stream of water from mountain springs. Then I
spotted it. I bent and picked up a piece of
more recent history; a large nut about an inch
and a half across the flats. As I peered at its
glorious rusty surface my mind raced back in
time to when thousands of tons of freight
rumbled over the tiny bridges that still cross
Mill Brook in places and thundered over iron
rails where I now stood; all held together with
this little metal man-made fastener I had in my
hand. Soon out of the corner of my eye I saw a
rusting washer and finally a bolt about four
inches long or so. After tapping a decade of
mucky moo out of the nut, why, the bolt and nut
still made a rather nice fit. The unlikely find
made my mind wander even further and I swear I
could actually hear the clickety clack of the
old Delaware & Hudson steamer. It's real
embarrassing to jump out of the way of an
imaginary train in chest waders waving a fly
rod, believe me. The hauling duties have now
been handed over to foul smelling diesel trucks
and ear splitting jet planes. The train era is
dead in large measure but on this roadbed the
old depot still stands in West Rupert. The

community uses it for storage and it even gets a
paint job and a sprucing up by volunteers now
and again. My mental trip to the past took me
about a quarter mile away from my truck which
made me regard the heavy rubber waders with
renewed interest; even emptied of water they are
a real package. I was sweating heavily now.
There's got to be a better way.

On subsequent hikes along the roadbed in
pursuit of fishing Mill Brook, I would find more
and more chunks of history in the form of
plates, bolts, nuts, washers, and spikes of
various sizes. In fact on one excursion I found
so many souvenirs I could barely carry them all
back to the truck along with my fishing rod
(rarely were there any fish to worry about). I
inquired at the general store in town and the
proprietor, Big John, told me the railroad hired
all the kids in town when they removed the
tracks to pick up the hardware. They paid a few
cents a pound. Apparently some of the kids were
like me, lazy, and picked up enough for a movie
ticket or some such and moved on.

I now have an old steamer trunk in the shed
half filled with these bits of nostalgia. At
least the shed will never blow away. When the
train era returns...I'm ready.

My Daddy used to say, "I'm not the engineer,
I don't drive the thing, why I don't even ring
the bell. But let something go wrong and see
who catches hell!"

CHAPTER 26

THE GREAT BACKLASH EVENT

Even prior to my tenth birthday I knew I was
good. In fact my dad had said many times I was
"the ___ ____ best at it".
I never spent much time on knots in the
Scouts like the other guys. Some of them knew
how to tie bowlines, square knots, sheetbends,
you name it. I only knew the granny and my
favorite specialty, the backlash. Every fishing
trip was a new, exciting opportunity to
practice. While other kids caught fish I
fabricated and disassembled backlashes; much
more challenging. I worked with braided nylon,
monofilament, any line weight and every type of
rod and reel combo. As I grew older my talent
became polished to a fine patina. I just got
better and better.

In fact that guy who bends spoons and nails
with telekinesis is fooling with kid's stuff.
What I can do with an electrical extension cord
at fifty feet is scary. A perfectly coiled cord
with plug at one end and a socket at the other
will jump into a tangle that will occupy the
next half hour or so to undo.

My friend and neighbor Ralphie Gilles picked
up on my aptitude and persuaded me to enter the
Great Backlash Event. It is held annually in
Connecticut in mid June giving the applicants
ample time to get back in shape after a winter
hiatus. Practice, for me though, is hardly
necessary. It's like riding a bicycle; you
never forget.

The big day came and I was really nervous as
I bellied up to the registration table to pick
up my entry number and T-shirt. I scanned the
competition and let me tell you, it was awesome.
Most were about my age but wore nasty, menacing
expressions. There was even a girl in the field
and she really looked tough. They all sort of
milled about with a large ball of monofilament
just alive with knots; each looked like a
probable winner and the contest hadn't even
begun!

My fingers wouldn't obey the brain as I
ineptly created a bird's nest that practically
fell apart of its own accord. A few of the
others observed my ineffectual practice casts
and I heard some sniggering. I was sure they
thought they had an amateur in their midst.
"Maybe that'll give 'em a big head," I thought
as I struggled to control my trembling hands.

Then, with mere minutes to go until the
start, the Head Judge reviewed the rules. There
would be no interference with other contestants,
no time outs, no laughing at other competitors,
once you've declared the backlash finished no
changing your mind and absolutely no do-overs!
The gun signaled the start and each challenger
cast the lumps of lead in their own fashion
allowing the line to overrun the reel. Heats
lasted four minutes apiece but most entrants
"declared" well before the time was up.

As the Judges attempted to unravel the
knots, the field was rapidly reduced to six.
New rods and reels were distributed, all
identical, and the second heat was underway.

On my left was a big fellow named Tom and as
he zinged his one ounce sinker into the air I
knew he'd be a tough one to beat.

On my right was the girl Judy Something-or-
other and she had pure style. My own attempts
rarely look graceful but I always thought that
an advantage in this sport. But Judy had grace.
I was certain she'd get all the style points and
me none. The rest of the lot were out of my
sight which always makes you nervous, you know?

The second heat was difficult but I managed
to survive to the third and final heat; for all
the marbles, as the say. Left standing were
Tom, Judy and Your's Truly. We were all eager
and confident. Tom wore a leering smile of
conceit and Judy just looked straight ahead with
determination; a well tuned athlete. I regarded
them both as bugs to be crushed; stepping stones
to victory!

I was psyching myself up to the biggest
bird's nest of a tangle seen in that county.

New rods and reels were once again passed
out; this time with only 1/2 ounce sinkers
attached. I knew this heat would be troublesome
as I whipped the cheap fiberglass rod with its
tin plated reel high above my head. I figured I
might, *just might*, have and advantage here as I
never owned anything *but* cheap fiberglass rods
and tin plated reels. I'd have felt more
comfortable, however, had the reel been rusty
and a few guides missing from the rod, matching
my own equipment. The gun suddenly went off and
it was fish or cut bait, so to speak.

I looped a high flyer for my first try as
Judy What's-her-name jabbed me with her elbow

while the Judge's head was turned. Definitely
out of line (no pun intended). As I doubled
over, however, a gorgeous bundle of knots was
forming in front of my very eyes. She said
something quite uncomplimentary and unlady-like
as her own toss landed almost knotless; just a
couple of laughingly simple snarls. Tom was
thrashing away and his confident smile had been
reduced to a mask of worry. I think they knew
even before the Judges' ruling that they had met
their match.

Then, finally, the Head Judge called out the
results; Tom...Nine Oh, Judy...Eight Five,
Al...Nine Five! A triumphant grin spread from
ear to ear as the reality sunk in. I had won
the Regional Great Backlash Event! My mind
swirled dizzily as thoughts of the Nationals
surfaced. Boy it sure pays to be good at
something. Maybe one day the Olympics!

And I've continued my quest for excellence,
baffling guides from New York and Vermont to
Montana and Wyoming. There's simply no stopping
me.

My Daddy used to say, "When you get to
feeling like one in a million, remember so is
the fat lady at the Circus.

CHAPTER 27

THE SECOND HOME

Certainly the last thing I wanted, ever, was
a second home. My primary residence on the Isle
of Long, in New York, has kept me wonderfully
busy for decades, what with cleaning the
gutters, writing checks for the utility bills,
toting gas cans for the lawn mower, pruning
trees and squirting the termites. No, I had in
mind a tiny cabin in the woods surrounded by
mountains, bristling with white pines and
maples, alight with wonderful setting suns,
invaded by bird songs and peacefully cool and
quiet at night. It would be a place of no real
magnitude and a place without worries of dents
in the aluminum siding. It would be a jumping
off spot for hunting, fishing, skiing, plinking
and even trapping; a sort of home base for a
sportsman, me, to use any time the spirit moved.
It would be Spartan in nature requiring only the
most minor upkeep. It would, in fact, be
heaven.

And somewhere in my lifetime I must have
done something right. I still don't know how
this could have happened given all my recorded
failures, mistakes and blunders but I was

offered a chance to buy a tiny log cabin in the
hills of Vermont snuggled dead center in a
valley between Shatterack and Egg Mountains
neither of which, thankfully, have ever been
famous for anything other than the fact that
they exist and produce timber. No ski areas, no
tramways, no nothing. The place was my dream
come true. It had a marvelous pond within
spittin' distance of the front door with a
lively, if small, population of brook trout,
frogs, salamanders and pond life of all kinds.
The pond was also totally irresistible to a kid
with a good skipping stone. At least my own two
boys could never pass it up. The trees offered
precious shade in the summer, firewood in winter
and maple syrup during the pre-spring season.
Also offered were logging roads which are simply
perfect for sledding on snowy winter days and
biking the rest of the year. They offer a real
treat as animals leave their record in tracks in
mud and snow. I could get up nice and early and
park myself alongside the roads with a Thermos
of hot coffee and watch the story of life,
played out every day, unfold around me. The
pond would provide entertainment year 'round
from fishing, swimming, boating in summer and
skating in winter. The cabin was complete with
a fireplace which would supply heat and
therapeutic flickering firelight. Cooking over
the fireplace on an open grill and simmering a
stew in a large cast iron kettle would be
something special. There was even an enormous
shed that would be just right for handcrafting
small items using only old-timey hand tools like
drawknives, spokeshaves, froes, cudgels, saws,
etc. Water comes from a terrific spring that
tastes better than an evening cocktail and is
icy cold all year. In short it was perfect and

we signed on the dotted line, or lines, as
everything is in triplicate in real estate.

And in fact the place, we call it Birch
Hills, has been just splendid, and everything we
hoped for. The first few years were peaceful
and just as described. Then came electricity
for convenience, several appliances, some power
tools and other electrical stuff we formally did
quite well without. Then mother insisted on a
telephone. The original "for an emergency"
seemed plausible but now the thing has become
another intrusion on the calm we used to enjoy.
An oil burner was added to take the chill off
when we arrived in winter, generally late at
night, and before the fireplace got going real
well. An electric pump seemed logical to
automatically draw that magic water from the
spring to the cabin on demand. A new roof
stopped some of the leaks that didn't bother us
at first. A power snow thrower and a
logsplitter were added to the arsenal. I drew
the line at television but it's nearly
impossible anyway nestled as we are between the
mountains. But we did, however, turn my little
hideaway, my sanctuary from the incredible
nonsense of today's living, into a "second
home".

So let me describe a winter trip I took
recently to my "second home" which used to be
simply a place to flop and enjoy. The weather
was cold; about 5 degrees. Fortunately the oil
burner popped on and began the slow process of
heating the little place. The rear wall is made
completely of stone as the cabin backs into the
mountain and it takes about three days for the
wall to stop sweating, not the thing you want to
bump into in your jammies let me tell you. I
leap into the crawl space, perform my usual
snake check and prime the electric pump. No go.

That's when I discover the batteries in the
flashlight did not survive since our last trip;
the beam of the flashlight begins a rapid
descent down to barely a glow. So with several
books of matches I approach the pump. It was
precisely at that time the oil burner quits.
The matches would now warm my fingers as well as
provide light. Two hours later with the pump in
several major parts I've rectified the problem.
A tiny pebble managed to get through the
strainer and jammed up the works. Now fixed, I
begin the laborious procedure of filling the
waterlines including the fancy hot water heater
(sissies right?). By now my hands are a deep
azure color and after resetting the oil burner
which, thank goodness, begrudgingly coughs back
to life, I spend twenty minutes in front of the
fireplace which my wife has cranked up using a
quarter cord of kindling; who cares? It is
apparent there is an odor about the place that
shouldn't be there. It is recognizable,
however, and the search for the dead mouse
begins with frequent stops by the fireplace to
get the blood to a tolerable viscosity.
    It was at this point my spouse announces
that the bathroom, a direct result of adding
running water, was as dark as the inside of a
boot. Blown fuse. Tracing the problem I find
that a mouse had chewed part way through the
wiring and expired in the attempt. This must
have occurred just as we were leaving on our
last visit. So two problems solved at once.
Repaired, and the lights burning gaily, I now
hear the unmistakable click of the thermal
overload in the refrigerator. So we move all
the food that could be frozen out to the shed
and the rest we eat. Another hour later I had
our hi-tech refrigerator humming but there was
little food to put in it. Meanwhile my bride

insists on starting the snow thrower to clear
the drive and a path to the cabin. Guess what?
Right, it didn't start and in fact has not
started to this day. After shovelling in the
dark we collapse, exhausted, to enjoy the two
low-tech items that never fail. They worked
when we still had a cabin and darned if they
don't work even with our "second home".

    The first is the fireplace which has no
moving parts, came with no service contract and
requires only periodic care and feeding from its
master. The second is a good book. This also
has no real moving parts and is absorbed by the
brain which I'm told, at least mine, has no
moving parts either. And when read by firelight
is about as relaxing as anything I can think of.

    I look back now and almost wish my "second
home" was still the little log cabin we started
with. We just had fun with no worries about oil
burners, telephones or electric gadgets. I
guess I'll just have to pop open a beer, sit by
the pond and dream of when we had less and
enjoyed it more.

    My Daddy used to say, "When you're up to
your knees in alligators it's hard to remember
you came to clear the swamp."

CHAPTER 28

THE MOUNTAIN TRUCK

It was just before hunting season several years ago I sat at the wood stove at Sherman's General Store with a rascal simply called 'B' and Tom, a dentist. We'd heard that Everett Duncan had a Jeep truck for sale. The Jeep was barely older than Methusala but the three of us, as partners, felt it offered some vague freedom inasmuch as we were in the habit of paying thirty bucks a pop to be plowed out after a snow storm, we could throw a plow on it and save money. And, since we hunted together, it would provide a way up the mountain in lieu of the usual hike. In fact there should be a full scale investigation into this matter of the trails getting steeper and longer each year. Something funny is going on here. So the Jeep would be a wonderful gentlemanly way for us to enjoy our sport. We all remembered, painfully, one attempt to take Tom's Buick up the mountain; the venture failed so thoroughly that we lost a whole day's hunting not to mention nearly losing the Buick. We pondered the very positive aspects of the plan. Our wives pointed out a negative or three that we somehow missed like

the extensive repairs needed, the upkeep, and
the fact that all three of us were near broke
(except Tom who still owned the rights to
several root canals).

Well, next day 'B' and I were contemplating
the significance of interstellar ions over a
malt drink at the store when in burst Tom
explaining that Everett had dropped the price of
the Jeep to $300, and if we kept the beast on
the log roads we wouldn't even need to register
it. Tom's opinion usually had more weight than
ours, him being a doctor and all, so the door to
our Mountain Truck Project began to open. I
could see things like loads of firewood coming
off the mountain with ease and trips to the big
nasty fish of Frost Hollow Pond deep in the
mountain woods. The door was now swinging wide.
Truthfully I'm no genius but 'B'...well I'll
give you an idea, last year I was going to get
him a book for Christmas but he said, "No
thanks, I already read one." 'B' only agreed to
the plan if we'd let him do all the repairs;
what a guy.

Of course incidental, non-funtional items
would not be repaired such as the missing
passenger side door, rear brakes, headlights,
windshield wipers, floorboards, etc. There was
enough important stuff to be fixed anyway. We
laid out an infant fortune for the clutch, a gas
tank sans hole, fuel pump, et al.

The Mountain Truck never did make it to
Frost Hollow Pond, not by a long shot, but we
did make one hunting trip in it. On opening day
We figured the Mountain Truck was as ready as it
could get on our combined budgets so we loaded
our gear and up the mountain we went, chosing a
logging road that looked pretty decent. I mean
a little mud and some ruts wouldn't be a
problem, after all, this was our Mountain Truck.

Tom Drove, 'B' sat in the passenger seat
clutching the dashboard so as not to be tossed
out through the void created by the missing
door, and I perched atop some of the gear in the
rear, serving as sort of a look-out. We got
about a half mile or so wallowing in some mud
filled ruts and slip-sliding our way along when
the look-out spotted our first significant
obstacle; a downed tree of goodly size.

We were prepared, however, and had a small
chain saw on the floor. We started her up and
in no time were cutting and moving branches and
logs out of the way. Soon after we began, ever
the look-out, I noticed the Mountain Truck begin
to roll backwards down the logging road, slowly
at first in the mud, then faster and faster as
the dry spots came up. I shouted to Tom, "You
forgot to set the parking brake!"

"Did not!"

"Did too!"

"Didn't; there ain't any parking brake!"

"Oh."

We chased the Mountain Truck for a good
stretch when, thankfully, it fetched up against
a big birch tree. We managed to get out of the
brush and back on the logging road after quite a
bit of effort. Finally passing the downed tree
once more we came to an intersection of two
roads. None of us had ever taken this
particular road so a discussion of left or right
ensued. With no logic to the decision at all we
went right. While the decision was being made
and our Mountain Truck idled fitfully it began
to overheat. We didn't get very far; the road
we chose was exceedingly steep and our Mountain
Truck didn't care for it much. Steam became
rather apparent, pouring out from everywhere it
seemed.

Stopping, 'B' got out and opened the rusty
hood only to be greeted with a scalding blast of
steaming coolant from a hole in one of the
hoses. The hood was dropped immediately and its
slamming caused the dislodging of several
traitorous parts from under the Mountain Truck,
not that there was all that much left to fall
off.

Without a word we each grabbed our gear from
the back of the Mountain Truck and began the
slow, laborious hike up the road to our hunting
spot. The expressions on our faces summed it
up. We had spent more energy getting only about
halfway up the mountain in the Mountain Truck
than when we would had we hiked the full
measure. It was only ten in the morning, we
were beat and not even where we wanted to hunt.

As far as I know the Mountain Truck is still
there. The episode has been relegated to
forgotten history (except for our wives who
occasionally recall the adventure and needless
expenditures on parts now peacefully rusting on
some logging road; usually these recollections
precede a notice that they are in need of new
shoes or coat).

Last week I sat once more with 'B' and Tom
at Sherman's working on some of the world's more
knotty difficulties when I reached down into the
cracker barrel. As I did I said, "Oh, by the
way, Everett says he's got an old Ford tractor
for sale. That'd sure get us up the mountain
come huntin' season." When I straightened up
both 'B' and Doc were gone. In fact I've gotten
the distinct feeling they've been avoiding me
all week. I still have to tell them he's
dropped the price to just $300; needs a little
work maybe, but if we keep to the logging
roads...

My Daddy used to say, "A man who can spot a bad idea before it gets there is wiser'n a tree full of owls."

CHAPTER 29

WAITERS AND WAITRESSES

I was originally going to call this account
"Waiters and Waitresses I Have Known" but I then
realized that sportsmen in pursuit of their
particular outdoor diversions seldom actually
get to know waiters and waitresses they meet;
except for Leslie, a special case which I'll get
to later. Mostly we're just passin' through or
at best on a very temporary stay. These folks
who portage victuals in restaurants and
roadhouses come in as wide a variety as hatches
on a stream but the sportsman prefers them to be
real people; guys and gals that can chat about
hunting and fishing...maybe archery...while
serving up steaming bowls of porridge. Fancy is
generally overkill and basically out of the
question. Just plain people will do nicely,
thank you very much.

One time I was hunting with two friends,
both professional men whose wallets are always
bulging with pictures of Ben Franklin. They
insisted we have dinner at a "nice little French
place" they knew. And so we went. I realized
right off this was not the place for me by the
look a guy called a "maitre d" gave my red

checked shirt partially covered by my Orvis
tweed sportcoat. We were seated at a table so
far away from other humans you'd need a bus to
get to the men's room which had some other
foreign name on the door; thank goodness for the
little icons on the door along with the French
stuff.

The waiter, resembling a six foot penguin,
arrived so silently at our table I took a quick
look to see if he was wearing shoes; indeed he
was, the shine made my eyes smart for several
minutes. I decided to have a glass of wine
before dinner and the penguin sneaked up on me
once again handing me a damp cork. Actually I
thought that very considerate. Cut in thirds
and shaped a bit they'd make nice bass bugs so I
stuck the cork in my pocket and said, "Thanks."
He mumbled something that sounded like "mercy'
that I didn't understand and seemed to be
staring at something on the ceiling.

I noticed that these fancy waiters don't
trust themselves all that much as this one
carried a towel slung right there on his arm in
case of a spill. But he didn't spill a drop,
I'll give him that. In fact all he poured at
first was a few drops. I thought this was kind
of chintzy considering the cost of the wine
alone would force me into next week's budget.
So being just a small quantity I was able to
down it in one gulp. Apparently Mr. Penguin
thought I'd passed some sort of test 'cause then
he filled the goblet right to the top. I told
him that was more like it but he'd already spun
around on his heel and was hoofing it away at a
good pace mumbling again.

He returned and handed out menus with
aplomb. They looked more like tiny billboards
they were so big but I guess that's because the
lighting was so poor. Anyway, my two comrades

were chatting away in French with the penguin,
discussing the fares on the menu I presumed,
which unfortunately came with no English
translation. I watched the encounter more or
less like a tennis match...back and forth, back
and forth. Whatever it was they ended up with I
decided to have the same. It turned out to be
duck with some sort of oranges or something and
boy! I couldn't wait; a sportsman sure gets
hungry.

Dinner came as the waiter slinked up to the
table once more and set down the plates with a
little turn; nice touch. Mind you, though, a
sportsman likes his waiters and waitresses to
make a little noise. I mean they don't have to
bang pots in your ear but, you know, a little
laugh never hurt, kind of shows they're alive.
I wondered if I would understand French laughter
anyway.

I had expected something I could sink my
molars into. I asked, "Yo, where's the rest of
it there Pierre?" The meal looked gorgeous but
very lost on the plate. He just smirked and the
bill looked like the cost to dismantle the
Golden Gate Bridge.

Now when they let *me* pick the restaurant I
know where to find the waiters and waitresses
that can spot a hunter or fisherman a mile away
and give you some down home chit-chat. First, a
sportsman's restaurant will always have two
letters missing from the neon sign announcing
the name of the joint. You can pretty much bet
the folks who ferry food in these places are not
graduates from the Culinary Institute but you'll
feel welcome and comfortable and, Lord, they'll
never sneak up on you. Then you look at the
parking lot. Don't even consider any
establishment with valet parking. Potholes are
a good sign, Cadillacs and BMW's aren't. Check

for pickup trucks as a good indication of a down
to earth spot with waiters and waitresses who
understand a hunter's appetite. Pickups with a
fishing pole in the back or a rifle in a rack
above the cab window are even better. When you
see this wonderful combination hurry in and
order; just watch out for the mounted moose head
above the door and, whether a fisherman or
hunter, be prepared to answer the inevitable
question, "Jagetny ?"

I mentioned that sportsmen seldom get to
know their waiters and waitresses and it's true.
There is an endless parade of nameless
faces...with the exception, in my case, of
Leslie. My pals, Mike and Joe, and I were
fishing with the Long Island Flyrodders on the
Willowemoc some time back and at the generous
invitation of Mike's long time friends and
residents of the area, Walt and Kathy, stayed at
their mountain castle which is within spittin'
distance of prime trout water. We fished a full
day in a downpour, keeping the Flyrodder's
record for rotten weather on their trips fully
intact.

That evening Walt suggested we dine at a
local bistro he said had exceptional food. Now
Walt knows the kind of waiters and waitresses
sportsmen prefer so the place, we knew, would be
perfect.

We entered the emporium smelling vaguely of
fermented rainbow trout (that is, Mike and Joe.
I make it a point never to catch fish on a day I
plan to eat out...or a day I'm breathing air for
that matter). We were seated at a central table
and as we did so, noticed the surrounding tables
were rapidly vacated.

In the background I noticed the waitresses
huddled in a rough circle drawing straws. The
lovely young lady, known eventually as Leslie,

came up with a straw that looked markedly
different in length from the others. Her
comrades offered sympathetic looks and with an
encouraging shove, forced her in the direction
of our table. As she came to a skidding stop I
realized right away she had picked me out as her
favorite when she pointed a beautifully
manicured index finger with a nail sharpened to
scalpel fineness at me and said, "You...shut
up!:" I learned later this was just Leslie's
way of saying, "have a nice day!" In fact she
bade me, "Have a nice day!" several times that
evening.

Walt made the proposal that perhaps, since
this was sort of an occasion, we all might have
a beer to celebrate. The occasion, of course,
was that Mike and Joe had caught fish virtually
all day long. I, on the other hand, enjoyed a
rather full day of casting practice in the rain.
Anyway we put it to a vote and ordered a beer
apiece which came in pretty green bottles. I
remarked to Leslie that the temperature of the
lager was possibly a few degrees warmer than
ideal at which point I caught a glimpse of a
whole handful of stiletto nails and got a mental
picture of same shredding the back of a shirt on
the way out the door. I wisely removed my
stream thermometer from the bottle and agreed
that a degree or two was nothing between friends
which I had hoped Leslie and I would become
before any real damage could be done. She bade
me, "Have a nice day!" and we ordered.

I had the "special" and thankfully it did
not contain any gooey red sauces as, while my
companions were served, more or less silently,
the slap of the platter on the table before me
actually woke a sleeping Monk some forty miles
distant at a Catskill retreat and put trout down
for a full three days.

I then ventured a request to our lady in serving and asked if I might have some more of those delightful rolls. She said, "Absolutely not!" Now I prize honesty above all else and Leslie was honest. Usually a waitress will say, "Why certainly," and then go off on a European vacation.

We left shortly thereafter and as we piled into Joe's van, Walt happened to ask, "Hey, Al, Why is your shirt ripped to ribbons in the back like that?"

My Daddy used to say, "If it were raining silver dollars, sure enough, they'd serve my bowl upside down!"

CHAPTER 30

REVENGE

Revenge, as we all can testify, can be ooooooh! so sweet. It starts at a very early age when finally we get the chance to watch the bully in first grade go nuts looking for his Donald Duck lunch box which you had the unexpected opportunity to hide behind the classroom radiator where his chunky peanut butter from his sandwich was at that very moment saying hello to his juicy apple now shrivelling up in his Snickers dessert puddle.

But revenge can have its own quirky convolutions.

I can offer no better evidence than the story of my three acquaintances Harry, Fred and Jim. All three, now comfortably in their forties, met as freshmen in high school and have for some reason stayed as a threesome for all these years; that is until fairly recently. Jim was the big athlete, three letter man, always gregarious, a girl magnet in school, and good at all physical sports. He is one of those folks who absolutely *must* come in first, score higher, lift heavier and go further than everyone else. A normally friendly guy, he could become

downright ugly if not winning. Fred, on the
other hand, is a bit introversive. A nice guy,
of course, but not a competitive animal like Jim
and back in school went out for no sports. He
had the average amount of dates, a fair sense of
humor, and paid more attention to his diet and
health than most of us. They'd have called him
a health freak back then except the phrase had
yet to be coined. Instead of pizza and chili
dogs he would consume an apple or two and a tuna
sandwich for lunch (back when tuna could be
bought without a mortgage). In fact we thought
it was he who invented tofu. Jim and Fred had
only one thing in common; they loved to pick on
and tease Harry and, by golly, Harry gave them
much to further their hobby.

Harry is...well Harry is Harry. You'd pick
him out of a crowded ballpark in a moment. His
hair would point all directions of the compass
and, for whatever reason he was being punished
by the gods, his face was unfortunately always
decorated by acne which minimized his dance
card. (the acne cleared in his Senior year and
the dates picked up proportionately). And he
wore glasses, possibly since birth. I mean *real*
glasses, thick as a storefront window and the
frames were perennially held together with
adhesive tape. Without his glasses Harry might
just as well have been on another planet. Harry
was, and still is, generous to a fault, a non-
complainer and always willing to offer
assistance to anyone who seemed to need it. As
a Boy Scout he got into a bit of trouble helping
a little old lady across the street as he was
told Scouts are supposed to do. The problem,
however, was she didn't really want to cross the
street. In the brains department Harry was not
a champion. It is rumored that he was recently
injured placing another log on the kerosene

heater. Harry had absolutely nothing in common
with either Jim or Fred except for being the
constant butt of their jokes which makes their
long lasting partnership, including hunting,
fishing, and camping trips, truly remarkable.
But last year something triggered in Harry's
head; he'd had it. It was time for a little old
fashioned revenge.

The trio planned a trip together in the late
fall. It was to be a three day affair combining
a camping excursion with a little squirrel
hunting. Even with his thick glasses Harry was
an excellent shot and would have gotten more
squirrels than either of the others on most of
their trips except Jim would never permit it and
would always have to go out and get one more.

The deal was they bring their own breakfast
preparations; eggs, oatmeal, like that. Lunch
would be squirrel meat (the pelts and tails
would be saved to tie next spring's flies). But
for dinner each of the lads were responsible for
bringing the fixin's for the whole group for one
day. This was very traditional, and further, it
was traditional that the meal choice be a
secret. This is how it has always been with
them. Jim and Harry were always afraid Fred
would show up with a few apples and yogurt so
this was against the rules; the dinner must be
cooked over an open fire and contain real meat
(not disguised soy bean curd or some such).

The first two days went well as far as the
camping and squirrel hunting went. As usual,
though, Harry took a ribbing day and night but
did not complain. In fact he wore a smile that
worried both Jim and Fred to the point that they
asked Harry if he felt ok several times.

This, now being the third day, and lunch
having just been completed, Jim and Fred left to
"check out a new area for hunting on a future

trip". Harry meanwhile, as always, cleaned up
the camp. Now the arrangements were that Jim
and Fred had a two man tent which they shared.
Harry also had a two man tent which he was
allowed to share with gear belonging to the
three of them. After doing the chores of camp
alone Harry entered his tent and emerged with a
good sized sack that seemed, well, almost alive.
He then entered Jim and Fred's tent and emerged
with an empty sack; the grin now more evident
than ever.

Actually I lied earlier, Jim and Fred have
one other thing in common; an inordinate fear of
snakes, a factoid not lost on our boy Harry.
The mere mention of the word "snake" has been
known to send them quivering. So what Harry did
was visit a pet shop specializing in such
critters and after absolute assurance that the
two large, brownish-black snakes in the window
were perfectly docile and non-poisonous (Harry
was not really a snake fan either) he purchased
same. With great care and a set of acrylic
paints, he made them look remarkably like
rattlesnakes down to the rings at the tail.
They would fool no one long but to someone
headed away from them at great speed they would
look real as could be. Now the place they were
camping, suggested by Harry, was known to be
inhabited, at times, by rattlers but Harry
convinced the others that, being late fall, they
would be quite dormant. The word sissy came up
and Jim and Fred finally agreed. After some
initial trepidation they soon gave no more
thought to snakes as they poked fun at Harry
during the trip.

When Jim and Fred came back, both smirking
at how they avoided clean up chores again, the
three set out to gather some wood for the
evening campfire to cook supper which assuredly

would not meet with the approval of Fred and Jim
as it was Harry's turn. Back at the camp with
dusk creeping in fast and the fire started Jim
and Fred entered their tent to get their
utensils and came bolting out at full scream,
snapping guy lines and tumbling over one
another. At Harry's query they shouted,
"Sssss...sssss...sssnakes! Rrrr...rrrr
...rrrattlers!"

Harry offered, "Geez, you guys are some
bunch of girls. I'll take care of it." And
with that he went into the half crumpled tent
and came out holding what appeared, at least to
two guys frightened out of their wits, a rattler
in each hand.

He then said, "Oh, by the way, I didn't
bring anything for supper tonight; forgot. So
we'll just roast up these two here."

Jim and Fred dove for the brush surrounding
the campsite and made vulgar noises that
indicated they may forego dinner and, in fact,
the rest of the trip. Pale, they cautiously
came from the bushes and proceeded to pack their
gear and prepare for the three mile hike down
the trail to their four wheel drive vehicle.
Harry always travelled separately as his
antagonists claimed there was only room for two
in their truck. Harry had cleverly parked his
own vehicle safely away from theirs.

Harry sat on a low stump and dropped the
snakes at his feet as he wiped tears of laughter
from his eyes watching the other two march down
the old logging road.

As his laughter dwindled to sporadic bursts
and he was alone he looked down by his feet and
said to himself, "Amazing what you can
accomplish with just three snakes. Three
snakes? *Three* snakes! **THREE** snakes...!!!"

My Daddy used to say, "You want the rainbow? Ya gotta accept the rain."

CHAPTER 31

JUST GOTTA GO

"Hey Al, goin' to the flyfishing show next weekend?", my fishing partner asked during a phone call recently. Actually the question was moot and the answer a foregone conclusion.

"Yeah, maybe," I answered knowing full well that a wagon load of beasties or being hit by a suburban bus wouldn't keep me away.

A flyfishing show is the catnip of the flyfishing sport. Why under one roof you can view and test all manner of new rods, reels, do-dads, and gadgets requiring an infant fortune or a lien on the old homestead to actually take ownership. And as for fly tying, there is enough fur, feathers and fluff to make about a thousand large, multicolored oriental rugs. The ticket prices on the flyfisherman's hardware has crept up at the modest pace reminding me of those logarithmic curves I allegedly understood back in high school. Yet there it will all be, in all their highly polished glory, gleaming and full of promise. The promise is that whatever piece of flyfishing gear you are looking at will solve some elusive problem keeping you from *really* big fish.

On an ordinary day my blood pressure hovers around 120 over 80. On the day I get the flyer announcing the next flyfishing show it soars to 160 over 100. Well known in medical circles, doctors refer to this as FFS Syndrome and will generally defer any serious testing until the week after the show; just to give a little settling out time.

The day of the Big Show this year found six of us piling into my pal Jack's large, user friendly van for the trip. The usual pre-show excitement had us occupied with conversations in which each participant had very precise ideas of what he wanted to see. Note here that none of us really *needed* anything. We've all been fly fishing for many years and have tied several lifetimes worth of flies, have a rod for practically any circumstance and reels with extra spools that have never even seen the light of day, *but*, you just never know what new gadget may appear and be found absolutely essential to catch, once again, the really big fish.

On board were sandwiches and adult beverages for the return trip. The CD player tossed out some tunes and the atmosphere was rather jovial as we unravelled some old tales of fishing trips and fishing shows of the past.

When we arrived at the door of the convention center where the Big Show was being held, the fever was on us and the five minute delay on line became unbearable. You were within spittin' distance of the bright lights, the fly casting pool, the sparkling trinkets on the tables, yet there you stand with your advance purchase ticket in hand waiting for a very unsympathetic ticket taker to get a move on. Ahead lay fly fishers' heaven; so near and yet...

Finally inside, along with the vast array of goodies to purchase and have for your very own, were fly tying seminars, casting demonstrations, slide shows on fishing trips and lots more to keep a fly fisherman occupied for a full day. You remind yourself one more time, "I do not need anything, I'm just looking and I'll take in the free seminars!" Every thing is just perfect.

Well, maybe not exactly. You go to the snack bar and wait twenty minutes on line for a cup of coffee, $1.00. You discover that a sandwich is $5 and a beer requires a mortgage. You look at the program handed out at the door and realize you just missed the slide show you dreamed about. And it seems each essential item you purchased was a buck less on the next aisle. Further, for a guy who absolutely did not need anything, as they usher you out at quitting time you have an empty wallet and a plastic bag full of stuff you already have. However, you thoroughly enjoyed the day and the trip home will be fun.

So, will I go back next year? Again a moot question.

My Daddy used to say, "Forget the chest pains, get me to the show!"

To order additional copies of **My Daddy Used To Say...**,

Send $10 per book to:

Westbrook Hi-Tech Services

PO Box 7123   Wantagh, NY   11793-0723

_____Copies of **My Daddy Used To Say...** @ $10 each $ _____

Total Enclosed $_____

Includes all taxes and shipping

Ship to: Name_____

Address_____

City, State, Zip_____

Please make checks payable to Al Westbrook

To order additional copies of **My Daddy Used To Say...**,

Send $10 per book to:

Westbrook Hi-Tech Services

PO Box 7123   Wantagh, NY   11793-0723

_____Copies of **My Daddy Used To Say...** @ $10 each $_____

Total Enclosed $_____

Includes all taxes and shipping

Ship to: Name_____

Address_____

City, State, Zip_____

Please make checks payable to Al Westbrook